This book belongs to

____

____

Program *of* Priestly Formation

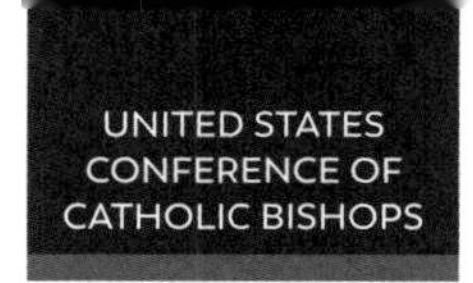

PROGRAM *of* PRIESTLY FORMATION

SIXTH EDITION

Local Norms for Priestly Formation
in the United States of America

The document *Program of Priestly Formation* (sixth edition) was developed by the Committee on Clergy, Consecrated Life and Vocations of the United States Conference of Catholic Bishops (USCCB). It was approved by the full body of bishops at its November 2019 General Meeting, received the subsequent *recognitio* of the Holy See, and has been authorized for publication by the undersigned.

Fr. Michael Fuller, STD
General Secretary, USCCB

Cover and Interior Design by: Ashley Dias

ISBN 978-1-954882-47-8

Published under license granted by the United States Conference of Catholic Bishops.

Ascension
PO Box 1990
West Chester, PA 19380
1-800-376-0520
ascensionpress.com

Printed in the United States of America
22 23 24 25 26 6 5 4 3 2 1

— CONTENTS —

Note: The numbers appearing at the top corner of each page refer to paragraph numbers of the text.

DECREE OF PROMULGATION

On November 12, 2019, the members of the United States Conference of Catholic Bishops approved the *Program of Priestly Formation in the United States of America* (sixth edition) as the *Ratio Nationalis Institutionis Sacerdotalis* for the United States to be observed in seminaries for the formation of priests.

This action of the United States Conference of Catholic Bishops, made in accord with canon 242 §1 of the *Code of Canon Law* and the *Ratio Fundamentalis Institutionis Sacerdotalis*, n. 3, was granted *confirmatio ad quinquennium* by the Congregation for the Clergy (Prot. N. 2022 0557), by a decree signed by Most Reverend Lazzaro You Heung-sik, Prefect of the Congregation for the Clergy, and Most Reverend Andrés Gabriel Ferrada Moreira, Secretary for Seminaries, and dated March 22, 2022.

As President of the United States Conference of Catholic Bishops, I therefore decree the promulgation of the *Program of Priestly Formation in the United States of America* (sixth edition), which is to be observed in all seminaries, whether diocesan or interdiocesan, effective August 4, 2023, the Feast of St. John Vianney.

Given at the offices of the United States Conference of Catholic Bishops in Washington, the District of Columbia, on the 24th day of June in the year of our Lord 2022 the Solemnity of The Most Sacred Heart of Jesus.

Most Reverend José H. Gómez
Archbishop of Los Angeles
President

Reverend Michael JK Fuller
General Secretary

FOREWORD

The development of this sixth edition of the *Program of Priestly Formation* (PPF) began with a review of the fifth edition by the Committee on Canonical Affairs and Church Governance, the National Association of Catholic Theological Schools, the National Association of College Seminaries and the National Conference of Diocesan Vocation Directors. Following the consultation of the full Conference at regional meetings of the USCCB, a request was made to the Congregation for the Clergy for a simple renewal of the *recognitio* for the fifth edition, which was granted on October 15, 2015. In December 2016, the new *Ratio Fundamentalis Institutionis Sacerdotalis* was released; in 2016, Bishop Michael Burbidge, Chair of the Committee on Clergy, Consecrated Life and Vocations (2013-2016), formed a working group to draft a new edition of the PPF.

The working group completed their work under the new Chair of the CCLV, His Eminence, Joseph Cardinal Tobin, C.Ss.R. (2016-2019). Members of the working group included Bishop Earl Boyea, Chair; Bishop Peter Baldacchino; Bishop Andrew Cozzens; Bishop Michael Olson; Bishop Thomas Paprocki; Msgr. Todd Lajiness; Msgr. Robert Panke; Rev. John Pavlik, OFM Cap; Rev. Tobias Rodriguez; Reverend Gladstone Stevens, PSS; and Rev. Jorge Torres, while Rev. Ralph O'Donnell, Rev. Luke Ballman and Rev. Daniel Hanley of the CCLV Secretariat supported the working group.

Following the completion of the draft, feedback from the CCLV Collaborating Committees and experts was incorporated into the text. The document was approved by the General Assembly in November 2019 and subsequently submitted to the Congregation for the Clergy for *recognitio*. Pope Francis modified CIC, c. 242 §1 *motu proprio* on February 11, 2022, changing *recognitio* to *confirmatio*. On March 22, 2022, Archbishop Lazzaro You Heung-sik, Prefect of the Congregation for the Clergy, and Archbishop Andrés Gabriel Ferrada Moreira, Secretary, issued the Decree confirming ad quinquennium the sixth edition of the *Program of Priestly Formation*. The Decree noted that the Conference, "welcoming the indications of the recent Magisterium, intends to offer candidates for priestly ministry a human, spiritual, intellectual, and pastoral formation achieved through an optimum community life and animated by a missionary spirit of evangelization that is congruous to the needs of the present age."

The members of the CCLV Committee who brought this project to completion are Bishop James Checchio, Chair; Archbishop Samuel Aquila; Archbishop Charles Thompson; Bishop Juan Miguel Betancourt; Bishop Earl Boyea; Bishop Ronald Hicks; Bishop David Malloy; and Bishop Daniel Mueggenborg. With the successful completion of this document, the Bishops' Committee on Clergy, Consecrated Life and Vocations is pleased to offer this *Program of Priestly Formation* with much gratitude for all those who participated in the project.

On behalf of the United States Conference of Catholic Bishops and the Committee on Clergy, Consecrated Life and Vocations, we thank all those who have worked throughout these six years on this effort. I also offer our prayers and support for all those who participate in the vital work of vocations and priestly formation. May Mary, Queen of the Clergy, ever assist us in this vital ministry for our Church.

Most Reverend James F. Checchio
Chairman, Committee on Clergy, Consecrated Life and Vocations

PREFACE

1 The documents of the Second Vatican Council[1] form an essential resource for the program of priestly formation along with the Council's specific treatment of priestly formation found in *Optatam Totius* (*Decree on the Training of Priests*). The teaching of the Second Vatican Council establishes the normative understanding of the presbyteral office. As authentic articulations of the Church's faith, these documents along with *Ratio Fundamentalis Sacerdotalis Institutionis* (*The Gift of the Priestly Vocation,* 2016), the Post-Synodal Apostolic Exhortation *Pastores Dabo Vobis* (*I Will Give You Shepherds,* 1992), the *Code of Canon Law* (1983), the *Code of Canons of the Eastern Churches* (1990), and the *Catechism of the Catholic Church* (1997) shape this current *Program of Priestly Formation.*

2 Other documents of the Holy See pertaining to priestly formation and treating specific aspects of seminary programs also contribute to this edition of the *Program of Priestly Formation,*[2] along with documents published by the United States Conference of Catholic Bishops (USCCB) and the Bishops' Committee on Clergy, Consecrated Life, and Vocations (CCLV) identifying particular concerns and giving specific directions in light of needs and experiences in the United

---

1 Among these, of special importance are *Lumen Gentium, Christus Dominus,* and *Presbyterorum Ordinis.*

2 The Holy See has given direction on the teaching of philosophy (1972), theology (1976), canon law (1975), mutual relations between bishops and religious (1978), liturgical formation (1979), social communications (1986), pastoral care of people on the move (1986), Oriental Churches (1987), social doctrine (1988), Mariology (1988), patristics (1989), formation in religious institutes (1990), marriage (1995), ecumenism (1998), *Fraternal Life in Community* (1994), and the interrelation of theology and philosophy (1998). The Congregation for Catholic Education has also commented on other aspects of formation, notably celibacy (1974), *Sapientia Christiana* (1979), and spiritual formation (1980). Additional documents of the Holy See that were issued following the promulgation of the *Program of Priestly Formation,* fifth edition, include Congregation for Catholic Education, *Instruction Concerning the Criteria for the Discernment of Vocations with Regard to Persons with Homosexual Tendencies in View of Their Admission to the Seminary and to Holy Orders* (2005); Congregation for the Doctrine of the Faith, *Minimum Profile of Formation for Former Protestant Ministers Who Desire to Be Ordained Catholic Priests* (2007); Congregation for Catholic Education, *Guidelines for the Use of Psychology in the Admission and Formation of Candidates for the Priesthood* (2008); Congregation for Catholic Education, *Decree on the Reform of Ecclesiastical Studies of Philosophy* (2011); and Pope Francis, *Veritatis Gaudium* (2017).

States.[3] The Bishops' Committee on Priestly Life and Ministry, one of the predecessor committees to the Bishops' Committee on CCLV, also contributed a series of important documents on priestly ministry and life that also has influenced this edition of the *Program of Priestly Formation.*[4]

3 The central focus of this latest version of the *Program of Priestly Formation* comes from reflecting on the lived experience of seminaries and the Church in the United States in these opening decades of the twenty-first century and takes its inspiration from the *Ratio Fundamentalis* published in 2016: "The fundamental idea is that Seminaries should form missionary disciples who are 'in love' with the Master, shepherds 'with the smell of the sheep,' who live in their midst to bring the mercy of God to them."[5]

4 This *Program of Priestly Formation* begins with an introduction to its central operating theme that priestly formation is an integrated journey, grounded in community and missionary in spirit. Building on this theme, the *Program of Priestly Formation* then explores the theological foundations of the ministerial priesthood, a description of the life of priests, and the Church's role in promoting priestly vocations. After this foundation, the text then outlines the process for admission into a formation program.

5 In the two chapters that follow those discussions, the text describes seminary formation. First is a discussion of the necessity of proper accompaniment. Here, the various people responsible for accompanying a seminarian through his formation are described. The next chapter sketches the structural elements of seminary formation,

3 These include documents, for example, on spiritual formation (1983), liturgy (1984), and pastoral formation (1985). Additional documents are *Preaching the Mystery of Faith: The Sunday Homily* (2013), *Guidelines for the Use of Psychology in Seminary Admissions* (2015), and *Guidelines for Receiving Pastoral Ministers in the United States* (2014).

4 These include documents, for example, on preaching (1982), stress (1982), sexuality (1983), general health of priests (1983), ongoing formation (1984), the role of pastor (1987), morale (1989), and a basic plan for the ongoing formation of priests (2001).

5 *Ratio Fundamentalis*, Introduction, no. 3.

beginning with the importance of integrating the dimensions (human, spiritual, intellectual, and pastoral) into the stages of seminary formation (propaedeutic, discipleship, configuration, and vocational synthesis). The goal of this integration is to aid the seminarian in cooperating with God's grace in conforming his heart as a disciple of Jesus Christ to the service of the Church in pastoral charity. The stages of seminary formation are then described in more detail. That chapter concludes with a description of the seminary community and the norms for evaluation.

6 Four chapters follow the chapter on seminary formation and present a detailed description of how each of the four dimensions (human, spiritual, intellectual, and pastoral), respectively, is to be integrated at each of the four stages of seminary formation (propaedeutic, discipleship, configuration, and vocational synthesis). Each chapter includes the benchmarks for that dimension, which the seminarian is expected to achieve before moving to the next stage.

7 This *Program of Priestly Formation* continues with a chapter about the ongoing formation of priests. This chapter is intended to help all those involved in the preparation of seminarians for the priesthood, including the seminarians themselves, to recognize that the seminary lays a foundation for a lifetime of formation. The USCCB, however, does have a separate document that presents ongoing formation in more detail.[6] The *Program of Priestly Formation* concludes with a section on seminaries that describes their governance, leadership, and personnel. The Program of Priestly Formation, then, is normative for United States seminary programs and serves as a basis for future visitations.[7]

---

6 USCCB, *The Basic Plan for the Ongoing Formation of Priests* (Washington, DC: USCCB, 2001). As of the publication of this *Program of Priestly Formation*, the *Basic Plan* is being revised; the second edition will be published soon.

7 See CIC, cc. 242, 455. This *Program of Priestly Formation* is intended to serve the entire Catholic Church in the United States. Some of its principles, norms, and pastoral applications are specific to the Latin Church. Nonetheless, the *Program of Priestly Formation* is also normative for all Eastern Catholic Churches *sui iuris* in the United States except where it conflicts with their particular traditions and pastoral life and with the requirements of the CCEO.

8 A Brief Note on Terminology: When the term "ecclesiastical entity" is used in this document, it refers to the diocese or eparchy, personal ordinariate, institute of consecrated life, or society of apostolic life for which a seminarian is preparing for ordained ministry in the Church in the United States. At the same time, each seminary, with the approval of the diocesan bishop or the bishops concerned, or of the competent authority of an institute of consecrated life or society of apostolic life as the case may be, is to develop, articulate, and implement its own particular program in conformity with the *Program of Priestly Formation.* The term "discerner" refers to a man who has not yet entered the propaedeutic stage and is in the process of discerning entry into the first stage of initial priestly formation. The term "seminarian" refers to a man who has been accepted into a seminary formation program. The term "candidate" refers to a seminarian who has received the Rite of Candidacy. The term "professor" refers to anyone who teaches courses, clergy and laity. The term "specialist" refers to a member of the formative community who is engaged in a specialized field (e.g., psychologist, counselor, librarian, business manager, and so on). The term "formative community" refers broadly to the larger community within the Church that is involved in varied ways in the discernment and initial formation of men preparing for the priesthood. It refers to the bishop and his priests and collaborators in the diocese and to all members of the seminary community, including priest formators, professors, specialists, other seminary staff, and above all, the seminarians themselves. It also refers to those engaged with the seminarian in his pastoral placements. Finally, it includes his family, parish, and others who are involved in his vocational journey. For members of an institute of consecrated life or a society of apostolic life, the term "formative community" includes members of his institute or society. The term "seminary community" is narrower in

meaning and refers specifically to the community of seminarians, priest formators, professors, specialists, and other seminary staff. The term "community of formators" is limited to those priests, both in the external forum and internal forum, who are engaged with the seminarian in his formation. The term "formator" is limited to priests. The term "biweekly" refers to an event that occurs every other week.

9 Care has been taken in this document to limit the use of prescriptive and exhortative language to two terms. The word "must" means that an action is required. Authorization from the competent authority is required for an exception from following the required course of action. The word "should" means that an action is highly recommended, such that a nonarbitrary reason is necessary for the decision not to pursue this course of action.

Introduction

PRIESTLY FORMATION: ONE, INTEGRAL, GROUNDED IN COMMUNITY, AND MISSIONARY IN SPIRIT

10 The journey of priestly formation begins at Baptism, when the new disciple of Jesus Christ begins to live the call to follow Christ in holiness. It is the same call disciples of Jesus have received since the foundation of the Church. St. John Paul II described seminary formation as "a continuation in the Church of the apostolic community gathered about Jesus, listening to his word, proceeding toward the Easter experience, awaiting the gift of the Spirit for the mission."[8] This singular "journey of discipleship," begun in Baptism, "comes to be appreciated as the center of one's life at the beginning of Seminary formation, and continues through the whole of life."[9]

11 Priestly formation is an integral journey in which the four dimensions of human, spiritual, intellectual, and pastoral formation are woven together in such a way that, while identified as distinct dimensions, they can be seen as an "integrated journey of the disciple called to priesthood."[10]

12 This integrated journey of discipleship is aimed at conforming the heart to the heart of Christ.[11] Being thus conformed to Christ leads the priest to pastoral charity, which animates all aspects of the life of the priest.[12]

13 The call to priesthood is essentially communitarian in nature. It is within the community of the family, parish, or ecclesial movement, or through interaction with an institute of consecrated life or society

---

8 *Pastores Dabo Vobis*, no. 60.
9 *Ratio Fundamentalis*, Introduction, no. 3.
10 *Ratio Fundamentalis*, Introduction, no. 3.
11 See *Ratio Fundamentalis*, no. 89; *Optatam Totius*, no. 4; *Pastores Dabo Vobis*, no. 57.
12 See *Pastores Dabo Vobis*, no. 57.

of apostolic life, that a vocation to priesthood is discovered. This vocation is discerned and nurtured within the seminary community. "This community leads the seminarian, through ordination, to become part of the 'family' of the presbyterate, at the service of a particular community."[13]

14 All Christians are prompted by the Holy Spirit to share the love of Jesus Christ with others; they are called to missionary discipleship. Baptism and Confirmation equip them to evangelize in all that they say and do.[14] Ministerial priesthood flows from this same call to missionary discipleship yet remains distinct.[15] The goal of priestly formation is to form missionary disciples so that they are ready for consecration as shepherds for God's People, sharing in the authority of Christ the Redeemer, who sent the Apostles to preach and heal.[16] In this way, priestly formation clearly must have a missionary character.[17]

15 Priestly formation today continues in the spirit of the response of the first disciples and their communion of life. The Gospel foundation of priestly formation precedes programs, structures, and plans. What was vital and essential for that first community of disciples remains so today for those engaged in priestly formation: "As he was walking by the Sea of Galilee, he saw two brothers, Simon who is called Peter, and his brother Andrew, casting a net into the sea; they were fishermen. He said to them, 'Come after me, and I will make you fishers of men.' At once they left their nets and followed him" (Mt 4:18-20).

16 The Church continues to place the highest value on the work of priestly formation, because it is linked to the very mission of the

---

13 *Ratio Fundamentalis*, Introduction, no. 3.
14 See *Evangelii Gaudium*, nos. 120-121.
15 See *Lumen Gentium*, no. 10.
16 See Lk 9:1-6, Mt 10:1-15, Mk 6:7-13.
17 See *Ratio Fundamentalis*, Introduction, no. 3.

Church, especially the evangelization of humanity:[18] "Go, therefore, and make disciples of all nations" (Mt 28:19). The apostolic origins of the Church, which bind all believers in communion with the Lord and his mission, motivate those who engage in the ministry of priestly formation, underscore the urgency of their task, and remind them of their great responsibility.

PRIESTLY FORMATION IN THE CONTEXT OF THE WORLD AND THE CHURCH TODAY

17 Priestly formation takes place in a given ecclesial and historical context. Identifying that context is a critical task for giving specific shape to particular programs of formation. The importance of context is highlighted in *Pastores Dabo Vobis*: "God always calls his priests from specific human and ecclesial contexts, which inevitably influence them; and to these same contexts the priest is sent for the service of Christ's Gospel."[19]

18 Worldwide, the current secular culture—"the economy of exclusion, the idolatry of money, the iniquity that generates violence, the primacy of appearance over being, postmodern individualism and globalization, as well as the reality of ethical relativism and religious indifference"[20]—presents many questions and challenges.

19 There are also many significant challenges, blessings, and opportunities that are particular to the United States in the twenty-first century. These play an important part in shaping seminary formation today. They also set the horizon for priestly ministry in the years ahead. Some of the more significant challenges are related to (1) American culture, (2) the Catholic Church in the United States, and (3) the discerners and seminarians themselves.

---

18 See *Pastores Dabo Vobis*, no. 2.
19 *Pastores Dabo Vobis*, no. 5.
20 *Ratio Fundamentalis*, no. 175.

20 (1) First, as it relates to American culture:

a. The United States is a nation with a rich cultural heritage of freedom, equality, justice for the oppressed, and open dialogue.[21] However, an "economy of exclusion and inequality" leaves many families trapped in a cycle of poverty.[22] Migrants and refugees fleeing hardship and violence continue to arrive in US communities. The evil of racism continues to be a factor in the social fabric of the United States; Catholic institutions are not immune to the persistence of racism in society.[23]

b. In most areas of the United States, the norm is a high level of cultural, linguistic, and economic diversity. Continued Catholic immigration has situated numerous newly arrived people, who present their own economic and religious issues, alongside numerous other Catholic laity who are native-born. Both groups share a common Church, have very different backgrounds, and can be mutually enriched by the exchange of their gifts.

c. In the United States at this time, there is the paradox of a widespread thirst for spirituality and, at the same time, a prevailing secular ethos. From another perspective, the nation finds itself more intensely called to build a "civilization of life and love," even as it struggles against a "culture of death." In United States society at large, many persons are unchurched or unaffiliated with any denomination or faith tradition but remain open to evangelization. So too, there is a growing number of persons, particularly young people, who are unchurched and who have rejected religious beliefs as irrelevant to their lives.

---

21 Pope Francis recognized this in his address to the US Congress during his 2015 papal visit: "A nation can be considered great when it defends liberty as [Abraham] Lincoln did, when it fosters a culture which enables people to 'dream' of full rights for all their brothers and sisters, as Martin Luther King sought to do; when it strives for justice and the cause of the oppressed, as Dorothy Day did by her tireless work, the fruit of a faith which becomes dialogue and sows peace in the contemplative style of Thomas Merton." Francis, "Visit to the Joint Session of the United States Congress" (address, US Capitol, Washington, DC, September 24, 2015), *www.vatican.va/content/francesco/en/speeches/2015/september/documents/papa-francesco_20150924_usa-us-congress.html* (accessed December 23, 2021).

22 *Evangelii Gaudium*, no. 53; see Francis, "Visit to the Joint Session of the United States Congress."

23 See *Evangelii Gaudium*, no. 53.

d. Weaknesses of ethical standards and a moral relativism have a corrosive effect on American public life as seen, for example, in marriage and family life, in business, and in politics.

e. The redefinition of marriage in culture and civil law and shifting understandings of gender and sexuality have transformed society such that the anthropological presuppositions that were once commonly shared are being called into question, making it more difficult for the seeds of the Gospel to take root and sprout.

f. Advances in technology have brought great progress to humanity but at the same time present new challenges.[24] These challenges are particularly present to young adults, who seem alienated from any authority or institution and who are accustomed to virtual relationships and constant recourse to social media. In addition, the widespread availability of pornography on the internet is a pervasive reality and a pernicious threat to human and moral development.

21 (2) Second, many factors within the Catholic Church in the United States also present opportunities and challenges that directly affect seminary formation:

a. The Catholic Church in the United States is reinvigorated especially by the new ecclesial realities born of the Second Vatican Council, which have offered a more positive context for vocations.

b. With a renewed sense of mission, the Church wants to engage in the new evangelization in these areas: evangelization through ordinary pastoral ministry, evangelization through ministry to the baptized who lack a relationship with the Church, and evangelization to those who do not yet know Jesus Christ or who have rejected him.[25]

---

24 "The gift of discernment has become all the more necessary today, since contemporary life offers immense possibilities for action and distraction, and the world presents all of them as valid and good. All of us, but especially the young, are immersed in a culture of zapping. We can navigate simultaneously on two or more screens and interact at the same time with two or three virtual scenarios. Without the wisdom of discernment, we can easily become prey to every passing trend." *Gaudete et Exsultate*, no. 167. See also *Laudato Si'*, no. 47; Pope Benedict XVI, Vespers Homily, Pastoral Visit to Lamezia Terme and Serra San Bruno, October 9, 2011, *w2.vatican.va/content/benedict-xvi/en/homilies/2011/documents/hf_ben-xvi_hom_20111009_vespri-serra-san-bruno.html* (accessed May 5, 2018).

25 See *Evangelii Gaudium*, no. 15.

c. The Catholic Church in the United States continues to be firmly committed to and engaged in ecumenical and interreligious dialogue and cooperation, something that "belongs to the very essence of" the community of the Lord's disciples.[26]

d. Globalization has underscored the need for greater coordination and deeper communion with the Church in other parts of the world. *Ecclesia in America* bears witness to this reality and responsibility, especially in our own hemisphere.

e. The ministerial collaboration of priests with bishops, other priests, deacons, men and women in consecrated life, and lay men and women is an important feature of the life of the Church in the United States.

f. The important presence and unique contribution of women in society and in the Church need to be acknowledged and nurtured. They offer an edifying example of humility, generosity, and selfless service.[27]

g. The demographics of the Catholic Church in the United States demonstrate the challenging situation of fewer priests and a large Catholic population.

h. There are large numbers of inactive or "semi-active" Catholics, as well as poorly catechized Catholics, who need to be called back to active participation in the life of the Church and, as needed, full initiation.

i. The cultural acceptance of the individual's right to exploration and expression of differences of belief brings Catholics in the United States into continuing and sometimes significant differences between their perceptions and the reality of what is essential to Catholic belief. These differences in perception strain many dimensions of the life of the Church and diminish the impact of the mission of the Church on society.

---

26 St. John Paul II, *Ut Unum Sint* (*On Commitment to Ecumenism*, 1995), no. 9, *www.vatican.va/content/john-paul-ii/en/encyclicals/documents/hf_jp-ii_enc_25051995_ut-unum-sint.html.*

27 See *Ratio Fundamentalis*, no. 151.

j. Within the Church, clericalism and abuse of power have had a corrosive effect. The scandalous and criminal behavior of some clergy who have abused minors and engaged in sexual misconduct with adults, including seminarians, has caused great suffering for the victims and damaged the Church's witness in society. This scandal has resulted in a loss of credibility for the Church and an overall lack of respect for religion. Both the nation and the Church are summoned to renewal and to a greater integrity of life. The *Charter for the Protection of Children and Young People and the Essential Norms for Diocesan/Eparchial Policies Dealing with Allegations of Sexual Abuse of Minors by Priests or Deacons* adopted by the Catholic bishops in the United States in 2002 (revised in 2005, 2011, and 2018) provide an example of moving in this direction. Also providing a way forward are the apostolic letter *motu proprio* of Pope Francis titled *Vos Estis Lux Mundi* (*You Are the Light of the World*) and the documents adopted at the USCCB's June 2019 general assembly.[28]

22 (3) Finally, the Church in the United States continues to benefit from the blessings that the variety of men in initial formation for priesthood bring. They also, as in every age, bring some unique challenges as well. The background of men preparing for priestly ministry also forms an important context for priestly formation in the United States.

a. They may be, for example, the following:

i. Men who are older and who bring previous life and work experiences

ii. Men born outside the United States who speak English as a second language

iii. Men whose faith has been rediscovered and rekindled in a powerful way through significant religious experiences, and men who are converts to Catholicism

28 See USCCB, "Directives for the Implementation of the Provisions of *Vos Estis Lux Mundi* Concerning Bishops and their Equivalents," "Acknowledging Our Episcopal Commitments," and "Protocol Regarding Available Non-Penal Restrictions on Bishops," in *A Continuous and Profound Conversion of Hearts* (Washington, DC: USCCB, 2019), 9-21.

iv. Men born and raised in the United States who find themselves struggling intensely with particular cultural counterpoints to the Gospel, especially regarding sexual permissiveness, the drive to acquire and consume material resources, utilitarianism, and the exaltation of freedom as merely personal and individual autonomy, divorced from personal responsibility and objective moral standards

b. An increasing number of priestly vocations now come from diverse and sometimes dysfunctional family situations.

The Ministerial Priesthood

INTRODUCTION

23 Christ instituted the ministerial priesthood to continue his work of salvation in the world. "The ministerial priesthood renders tangible the actual work of Christ, the Head, and gives witness to the fact that Christ has not separated Himself from his Church; rather He continues to vivify her through his everlasting priesthood."[29] All priestly formation must have its foundation in an adherence to the truths of faith about the nature and mission of the ministerial priesthood. Members of the seminary community who are involved in the process of priestly formation must adhere to these teachings. The priest is called to serve the great work of evangelization which Christ has entrusted to his Bride, the Church.

> Without priests the Church would not be able to live that fundamental obedience which is at the very heart of her existence and her mission in history, an obedience in response to the command of Christ: "Go therefore and make disciples of all nations" (Mt 28:19) and "Do this in remembrance of me" (Lk 22:19; cf. 1 Cor 11:24), i.e., an obedience to the command to announce the Gospel and to renew daily the sacrifice of the giving of his body and the shedding of his blood for the life of the world.[30]

TRINITARIAN FOUNDATION

24 The mission of the priest flows from his identity. The identity of the priest, like that of every Christian, is fundamentally rooted in a relationship with the Trinity. "It is within the Church's mystery, as a mystery of Trinitarian communion in missionary tension, that every Christian identity is revealed, and likewise the specific identity of the priest and his ministry."[31]

---

29 Congregation for the Clergy, *Directory on the Ministry and the Life of Priests* (Vatican City: Libreria Editrice Vaticana, 2013), no. 1, *www.vatican.va/roman_curia/congregations/cclergy/documents/rc_con_cclergy_doc_31011994_directory_en.html.*

30 *Pastores Dabo Vobis*, no. 1.

31 *Pastores Dabo Vobis*, no. 12.

> Indeed, the priest, by virtue of the consecration which he receives in the sacrament of orders, is sent forth by the Father through the mediatorship of Jesus Christ, to whom he is configured in a special way as head and shepherd of his people, in order to live and work by the power of the Holy Spirit in service of the Church and for the salvation of the world. . . . Consequently, the nature and mission of the ministerial priesthood cannot be defined except through this multiple and rich interconnection of relationships which arise from the Blessed Trinity and are prolonged in the communion of the Church, as a sign and instrument of Christ, of communion with God and of the unity of all humanity.[32]

The Church has "a responsibility to be a living sign of the Father's love in the world,"[33] a responsibility which the priest assumes as his own upon ordination. In this way priests "are visible signs of the merciful love of the Father in the Church and in the world."[34]

CHRISTOLOGICAL NATURE

25 For the priest to understand his identity, he must understand two central relations: his relationship with Christ, the Son of the Father, and his relationship with the Church. The primary point of reference for priestly identity is Christ himself: "The priest finds the full truth of his identity in being a derivation, a specific participation in and continuation of Christ himself, the one high priest of the new and eternal covenant. The priest is the living and transparent image of Christ the priest."[35] As priests "are configured to Christ, Head and Shepherd, Servant and Spouse,"[36] they

> are called to prolong the presence of Christ, the One High Priest, embodying his way of life and making him visible in the midst of the flock entrusted to their care. . . . In the Church and on behalf of the Church, priests are a sacramental representation of Jesus Christ—the

32 *Pastores Dabo Vobis*, no. 12.
33 *Misericordiae Vultus*, no. 4.
34 *Ratio Fundamentalis*, no. 35.
35 *Pastores Dabo Vobis*, no. 12.
36 *Ratio Fundamentalis*, no. 35.

head and shepherd—authoritatively proclaiming his word, repeating his acts of forgiveness and his offer of salvation—particularly in baptism, penance, and the Eucharist, showing his loving concern to the point of a total gift of self for the flock, which they gather into unity and lead to the Father through Christ and in the Spirit. In a word, priests exist and act in order to proclaim the Gospel to the world and to build up the Church in the name and person of Christ the head and shepherd.[37]

Calling to mind the image of the suffering servant (Is 53:4ff.), we are reminded that priestly ministers are called to embody the life of Christ, who accepted suffering and death as part of his mission to bring salvation to the whole world.[38] Because the priest is objectively configured to Christ through ordination, he must seek to make a personal gift of his life in response to this consecration.[39] The sacramental configuration to Christ the Servant was also conferred on the priest at his diaconate ordination. This configuration is not lost when he is ordained a priest but rather continues in imitation of Christ, who came not "to be served but to serve and to give his life as a ransom for many" (Mt 20:28).

26 Finally, Christ is the Bridegroom, a title which "expresses the truth about the love of God who 'first loved us' (cf. 1 Jn 4:19) and who, with the gift generated by this spousal love for man, has exceeded all human expectations: 'He loved them to the end' (Jn 13:1)."[40] "Hence Christ stands 'before' the Church and 'nourishes and cherishes her' (Eph 5:29), giving his life for her. The priest is called to be the living image of Jesus Christ, the spouse of the Church. Of course, he will always remain a member of the community as a believer alongside his other brothers and sisters who have been called by the Spirit, but

37 *Pastores Dabo Vobis*, no. 15.
38 See *Lumen Gentium*, nos. 14-16.
39 See *Ratio Fundamentalis*, no. 39.
40 St. John Paul II, *Mulieris Dignitatem* (*On the Dignity and the Vocation of Women on the Occasion of the Marian Year*, 1988), no. 25, *www.vatican.va/content/john-paul-ii/en/apost_letters/1988/documents/hf_jp-ii_apl_19880815_mulieris-dignitatem.html*.

in virtue of his configuration to Christ, the Head and Shepherd, the priest stands in this spousal relationship with regard to the community."[41]

27 This Christological foundation is particularly important for the life of the celibate priest. By the grace of the virtue of celibate chastity, a priest is a sign of the chastity of Christ. Formation for living priestly celibacy should take the chastity of Christ as a point of reference at every stage in all of its dimensions. As Pope Benedict XVI affirms, "The fact that Christ himself, the eternal priest, lived his mission even to the sacrifice of the Cross in the state of virginity constitutes the sure point of reference for understanding the meaning of the tradition of [priestly celibacy in] the Latin Church."[42]

ECCLESIOLOGICAL EXPRESSION

28 The second point of reference for priestly identity, following the priest's relationship with Christ, is his relationship to the Church. "As a mystery, the Church is essentially related to Jesus Christ. She is his fullness, his body, his spouse."[43] The priest's specific configuration to Christ brings about this special relationship to his Body, the Church. Within the Body, he represents Christ, Head and Shepherd, Servant and Spouse, as a co-worker with the bishop. The nature and mission of the ministerial priesthood can only be fully understood within the mystery of the Church, "as a service to the glory of God and to the brothers and sisters in their baptismal priesthood."[44] "The ministry of the priest," then, "is entirely on behalf of the Church; it aims at promoting the exercise of the common priesthood of the entire People of God."[45] To understand who he is, and therefore how he should live, the priest must understand himself in relationship

41 *Pastores Dabo Vobis*, no. 22.
42 *Sacramentum Caritatis*, no. 24.
43 *Pastores Dabo Vobis*, no. 12.
44 *Ratio Fundamentalis*, no. 31.
45 *Pastores Dabo Vobis*, no. 16.

with the Church. His participation in Christ's priesthood is called "ministerial" precisely for its service to the members of the Body.

29 *Pastores Dabo Vobis* expands our understanding of the ecclesiological scope of the ministerial priesthood by noting that it "is ordered not only to the particular Church but also to the universal Church, in communion with the bishop, with Peter and under Peter. Through the priesthood of the bishop, the priesthood of the second order is incorporated in the apostolic structure of the Church. In this way priests, like the Apostles, act as ambassadors of Christ (cf. 2 Cor 5:20). This is the basis of the missionary character of every priest."[46]

PRIESTHOOD IN PRESBYTERAL COMMUNION

30 These Trinitarian, Christological, and ecclesiological dimensions give us a sense of the nature, mission, and ministry of priests. It is important, however, to add that these dimensions only become real and operative in a presbyterate, one that is in communion with its bishop. "By its very nature, the ordained ministry can be carried out only to the extent that the priest is united to Christ through sacramental participation in the priestly order, and thus to the extent that he is in hierarchical communion with his own bishop. The ordained ministry has a radical 'communitarian form' and can only be carried out as a 'collective work.'"[47] This "communitarian form" also means that priests are to develop and foster bonds of fraternity and cooperation among themselves, so that the reality of the presbyterate may take hold of their lives.[48] Furthermore, seminaries and houses of initial formation are encouraged to foster mutual relations among members of institutes of consecrated life, societies of apostolic life, and seminarians in formation for the diocesan priesthood, so as to lay the foundation for a spirit of unity among future priests and ministers of the Church.

46 *Pastores Dabo Vobis*, no. 16.
47 *Pastores Dabo Vobis*, no. 17.
48 See *Presbyterorum Ordinis*, no. 8; CIC, c. 275 §1; CCEO, c. 379.

31 Priestly ministry, whether lived out in a particular Church or in an institute of consecrated life or society of apostolic life, can appear to be very different: one more geographically and parishbound, the other wider-ranging and rooted in a particular charism. Still, all priests share a common ministerial priesthood, belong to a presbyterate in communion with the diocesan bishop, and serve the same mission of the Church.[49] A common sacramental bond links all priests, although particular circumstances of ministry and life may be diverse. It is, therefore, essential for all priests and those in priestly formation to understand and to see themselves as engaged in the Church's ministry, subject to the same formation laid out in the *Program of Priestly Formation.*[50] Depending on the type of ecclesiastical entity, the details for the stages of formation may differ. For example, the propaedeutic stage for institutes of consecrated life or societies of apostolic life is handled by the postulancy or novitiate. In all cases the applicant, postulant, and so on must meet the benchmarks as noted in each dimension later in this document.

PRIESTHOOD: A JOURNEY OF DISCIPLESHIP

32 Discipleship is a lifelong journey of following Jesus Christ; this is certainly the case for the priest. Throughout his initial and ongoing formation, he continually learns to listen more attentively to the voice of the Master who calls him. Thus, formation serves him best when it can be experienced as an ever-advancing journey of conversion and growth. Gradually, as a disciple on this journey, he is able to make decisions that are permanent and that he will always be called upon to deepen and expand. The first stage of initial formation is the propaedeutic stage. During this stage, the man is introduced to the life of the Church as a community in which excellence of character

---

49 "It is of great importance that all priests, whether diocesan or regular [religious], should help each other, so that they may be fellow-helpers of the truth. Each is joined to the rest of the members of this priestly body by special ties of apostolic charity of ministry and of brotherhood." *Presbyterorum Ordinis*, no. 8.

50 This means not only that diocesan priests form a presbyterate, but that "religious clergy who live and work in a particular church also belong to the one presbyterate, albeit under a different title." *Pastores Dabo Vobis*, no. 74.

is nurtured, to the practice of daily participation in the Holy Mass, to love for Sacred Scripture, to the prayer of the Church (the Divine Office, or the Divine Praises in the Eastern Catholic Churches), and to the basic elements of the Christian faith as he discerns attentively and purposefully his potential vocation to priesthood in the presence of a supportive community of fellow seminarians and formators. This community is an ideal environment for growth in self-knowledge. In the discipleship stage, systematic formation as a disciple of Jesus Christ is the aim. The seminarian develops his principal strengths and grows to identify, acknowledge, and begin to overcome his shortcomings. In the configuration stage, the seminarian hones his capacity to serve and become a man for others. In the vocational synthesis stage,[51] the transitional deacon experiences a life of self-giving in a pastoral setting, as he begins the transition to full-time ministry.

33 This journey of discipleship and growth in Christian faith and service continues after ordination with ongoing formation, in which the ordained priest seeks an ever-deepening conformity to Christ under the guidance of the diocesan bishop or competent authority of the institute of consecrated life or society of apostolic life and in fraternal communion with the diocesan presbyterate and, in the case of nondiocesan priests, the presbyterate within his community.[52]

34 The human, spiritual, intellectual, and pastoral dimensions of formation are present in each stage and "must be seen through a unifying lens. . . . Together, these dimensions give shape and structure to the identity of the seminarian and the priest, and make him capable of that 'gift of self to the Church,' which is the essence

51 Throughout this document the term "vocational synthesis" is used to identify the last stage of initial formation, described in the *Ratio Fundamentalis* as "the 'pastoral stage' or 'stage of vocational synthesis.'" *Ratio Fundamentalis*, no. 57.

52 "Every priest should always feel that he is a disciple on a journey, constantly needing an integrated formation, understood as a continuous configuration to Christ." *Ratio Fundamentalis*, Introduction, no. 3.

of pastoral charity. The entire journey of formation must never be reduced to a single aspect to the detriment of others, but it must always be an integrated journey of the disciple called to priesthood."[53]

35 Community is an integral aspect of formation.[54] The gift of vocation appears in a Christian community; it is fostered and developed in the seminary community, with a view to serving the People of God in the community of the presbyterate.[55] The community of formators serves as a living model for the wider seminary community by "sharing a common responsibility, with due regard to the duties and the office entrusted to each member."[56]

36 Finally, the missionary aspect of formation emerges from the ecclesial dimension of the ministerial priesthood, directed toward the growth of the Church. "Formation is clearly missionary in character. Its goal is participation in the one mission entrusted by Christ to His Church, that is evangelization, in all its forms."[57]

---

53 *Ratio Fundamentalis*, Introduction, no. 3.
54 See *Ratio Fundamentalis*, Introduction, no. 3.
55 See *Ratio Fundamentalis*, Introduction, no. 3.
56 *Ratio Fundamentalis*, Introduction, no. 3.
57 *Ratio Fundamentalis*, Introduction, no. 3.

The Life *of* Priests

37 When the Second Vatican Council's decree *Presbyterorum Ordinis* speaks of "the life of priests," it refers to the whole of their existence but especially to the spiritual dimension that is at the center of all life. In a world that is increasingly secular in its outlook, it is especially important to note and hold fast to the one necessary thing (see Lk 10:42).

38 Along with all the baptized who have been given new life in Christ by the power of the Holy Spirit, priests are called with their brothers and sisters to live out their baptismal call as disciples of Jesus Christ and to grow in holiness.[58] While growth in discipleship is a lifelong journey, seminary formation is a privileged time for the future priest to discover that he is a "mystery to himself."[59] He will need to discover his talents and gifts and to recognize his limits and frailty, so that "the vocation to the priesthood does not become imprisoned in an abstract ideal, nor run the risk of reducing itself to a merely practical and organizational activism, removed from the conscience of the person."[60]

39 At the same time, priests are called to a specific vocation to holiness in virtue of their new consecration in the Sacrament of Holy Orders, a consecration that configures them to Christ the Head and Shepherd, Servant and Spouse. This configuration to Christ, a sacramental character effected by the Holy Spirit, prepares the priest for the mission and ministry which is specific to him[61] and which obliges him to be a "living instrument of Christ the eternal priest" and to act "in the name and in the person of Christ himself" and with his entire

58 See *Lumen Gentium*, nos. 39-42; *Pastores Dabo Vobis*, no. 20; CIC, c. 210; and CCEO, c. 13.
59 *Ratio Fundamentalis*, no. 28.
60 *Ratio Fundamentalis*, no. 43.
61 See *Catechism of the Catholic Church*, no. 1563.

"life," called to witness in a fundamental way to the "radicalism of the Gospel."[62]

40 For priests, the specific arena in which their spiritual life unfolds is their exercise of ministry in fulfillment of their mission.[63] The life of priests in the Spirit means their continuous transformation and conversion of heart centered on the integration or linking of their *identity* as configured to Christ, Head and Shepherd, Servant and Spouse, with their *ministry* of Word, Sacrament, and pastoral governance (leadership).[64] "In contemplating the Lord, who offered His life for others, he will be able to give himself generously and with self-sacrifice for the People of God."[65] He will more closely imitate Jesus, who came to serve and not to be served.

41 The ministry itself, by which the priest brings Christ's redemptive gifts to his people, transforms the priest's own life. In a particular way, the celebrations of the sacraments lead the priest to a holy encounter with God's all-transforming, merciful love.

42 When the priest's identity as sacramentally configured to Christ culminates in his ministry on behalf of Christ, which is called *amoris officium* (a work of love), he finds his unity of life in pastoral charity. "Priests will achieve the unity of their lives by joining themselves with Christ in the recognition of the Father's will and in the gift of themselves to the flock entrusted to them. In this way, by adopting the role of the good shepherd they will find in the practice of pastoral charity itself the bond of priestly perfection which will reduce to unity their life and activity."[66]

---

62 *Pastores Dabo Vobis*, no. 20.

63 See *Pastores Dabo Vobis*, no. 24; *Presbyterorum Ordinis*, no. 12; Synod of Bishops, *The Ministerial Priesthood and Justice in the World* (1971), part 2, I, iii.

64 See *Pastores Dabo Vobis*, nos. 24-26.

65 *Ratio Fundamentalis*, no. 41.

66 *Presbyterorum Ordinis*, no. 14.

43 Priestly life lived in configuration to Jesus Christ must necessarily manifest and give witness to the radicalism of the Gospel. In other words, priests are called to a way of life that gives evident and transparent witness to the power of the Gospel at work in their lives. A life of continual conversion allows the priest to become and remain "a 'man of discernment,' able to read the reality of human life in the light of the Spirit. In this way he will be able to choose, decide and act according to the will of God."[67] The elements of such a lifestyle—named here and to be developed elsewhere in this document—include the following:

a. A way of life permeated by the threefold charge given priests at ordination to teach, to sanctify, and to govern[68]

b. A life of steady prayer centered first and foremost on Sacred Scripture and the prayerful celebration of the sacraments, especially Penance and the Eucharist,[69] the Liturgy of the Hours (the Divine Praises, in the Eastern Catholic Churches), and the liturgical cycles, but also on devotional and contemplative prayer[70]

c. "Living intimately united" to the person of Jesus Christ, Lord and Savior, Son of God and Son of Mary[71]

d. Devotion to Mary, the Mother of God and Mother of priests[72]

e. A life of obedience that is apostolic, communal, and pastoral[73]

f. A life lived in communion with one's bishop and the presbyterate, a communion that includes sacramental, apostolic, and fraternal bonds[74]

g. For priests who are members of a religious institute or a society of apostolic life, a life in community with one's confreres in accord with the institute's Rule of Life and charism or with the constitution of the society of apostolic life

67 *Ratio Fundamentalis*, no. 43.
68 See *Presbyterorum Ordinis*, nos. 4-6, 13; *Pastores Dabo Vobis*, no. 26; *Optatam Totius*, no. 21.
69 See *Ecclesia de Eucharistia*, no. 31.
70 See *Pastores Dabo Vobis*, no. 33.
71 See *Pastores Dabo Vobis*, no. 46.
72 See CIC, c. 246 §3; CCEO, c. 346 §2, 5°.
73 See *Pastores Dabo Vobis*, no. 28.
74 See *Sacrosanctum Concilium*, no. 26; *Presbyterorum Ordinis*, nos. 7-8, 14; *Pastores Dabo Vobis*, no. 17.

h. A life of celibate chastity that serves both as "a sign and stimulus of love, and as a singular source of spiritual fertility in the world"[75] and, being freely accepted, shows that the priest is "consecrated in a new way to Christ"[76] and offers in himself a reflection of the chaste love of Christ for the Church[77]

i. A "simple and austere lifestyle"[78] that cares for and is in solidarity with the poor, works for universal justice for all those who are in need, and, with gratitude for the material blessings of God's creation, administers the goods of the community with utmost honesty and offers a courageous prophetic witness in the world[79]

j. A life that embraces "the mind and heart of missionaries open to the needs of the Church and the world"[80]

k. A life that promotes the array of ecclesial vocations[81]

44 The diocesan priest entrusted with the care of souls in many ways normally serves in parochial ministry. In the parish he will encounter the day-to-day joys and sorrows of the faithful as he accompanies them throughout life, continually leading them to encounter Christ. This art of accompaniment, which develops in the heart of the seminarian and continues to deepen in the heart of the priest, allows him lovingly to accompany the flock entrusted to him; he thus becomes a spiritual father to his people.

45 The life of priests in religious institutes and societies of apostolic life encompasses everything that has been said about the life of priests generally. It also adds to the exercise of the ministerial priesthood the distinctive aspects of a religious institute's Rule of Life or of the

75 *Lumen Gentium*, no. 42. See *Presbyterorum Ordinis*, no. 16.
76 *Ordination of a Bishop, of Priests, and of Deacons*, no. 177.
77 See *Presbyterorum Ordinis*, no. 16; CIC, c. 277 §1; CCEO, c. 374.
78 *Pastores Dabo Vobis*, no. 29.
79 See *Pastores Dabo Vobis*, no. 30; CIC, cc. 282, 287 §1; CCEO, cc. 385 §1, 384 §1. Pope Francis reminds us that "the natural environment is a collective good, the patrimony of all humanity and the responsibility of everyone. If we make something our own, it is only to administer it for the good of all." *Laudato Si'*, no. 95.
80 *Pastores Dabo Vobis*, no. 32. See St. John Paul II, *Redemptoris Missio* (*On the Permanent Validity of the Church's Missionary Mandate*) (Washington, DC: USCCB, 1990), nos. 15-16; CIC, cc. 245, 257; CCEO, c. 352 §3.
81 CIC, cc. 233, 275 §2; CCEO, cc. 329 §1, 2°, 381 §3.

constitution of a society of apostolic life. These aspects include the spirituality of the institute or society, common life, and distinctive apostolates that witness to the community's charism as a gift of the Spirit to the Church. Priestly formation for those men belonging to a form of consecrated life must therefore always situate the vocation to the priesthood within the charism and thus reference the spirituality, history, and mission of the particular institute of consecrated life or society of apostolic life, with fidelity to its founder, the institute's or society's mission, and the Church which receives that charism.

46 The primary context of priesthood for members of an institute of consecrated life or society of apostolic life ordinarily comes from the nature of the life itself as a deepening and fulfillment of a baptismal commitment to Christ by observing the evangelical counsels in an institute of consecrated life or a society of apostolic life approved by the Church.[82] Those men belonging to an institute of consecrated life or society of apostolic life who are called to priesthood exercise that ministry within the context of their institute or society. "In reality, the charism of the religious life, far from being an impulse born of flesh and blood or one derived from a mentality which conforms itself to the modern world, is the fruit of the Holy Spirit, who is always at work within the Church."[83] The exercise of priesthood takes on a distinctive quality for a man who belongs to an institute of consecrated life or a society of apostolic life, depending upon the Rule of Life, constitution, and charism of a particular institute or society. Nevertheless, the priest always exercises his ministry in union with the diocesan bishop as his co-worker.[84]

47 To a great extent, the deeper identification of those in consecrated life with the charism of their community's founder is due to their

82 "By the profession of the evangelical counsels *the characteristic features of Jesus*—the chaste, poor and obedient one—*are made constantly 'visible' in the midst of the world* and the eyes of the faithful are directed towards the mystery of the Kingdom of God already at work in history, even as it awaits its full realization in heaven." *Vita Consecrata*, no. 1.

83 *Evangelica Testificatio*, no. 11.

84 See *Ratio Fundamentalis*, no. 35.

obedience to the directives of the Second Vatican Council. "The up-to-date renewal of the religious life comprises both a constant return to the sources of the whole of the Christian life and to the primitive inspiration of the institutes, and their adaptation to the changed conditions of our time."[85]

48 Centuries of tradition bear witness to a difference between formation for the consecrated life and formation of seminarians for the priesthood. Formation for the consecrated life ordinarily precedes formation for priestly ministry—as an institute of consecrated life or society of apostolic life joyfully accepts its responsibility to form a man into its charism, and as the man owns and expresses the joy of the Gospel in the Rule of Life of the institute or constitution of the society—and accompanies a man in deepening his desire to serve Christ through ministerial priesthood. Aspects of formation to the priesthood that are addressed in the propaedeutic stage are addressed within early stages of consecrated life, that is, candidacy, postulancy, novitiate, and the time of temporary profession when a foundation is laid for public witness to the evangelical counsels as expressed in a particular institute or society. Nevertheless, the religious institute or society of apostolic life also assumes responsibility for forming the man for Holy Orders according to the mind of the Church and thus recognizing the human, spiritual, intellectual, and pastoral requirements incumbent upon all who are called to ministerial priesthood, and how these exist in addition to the formation for the consecrated life itself.

49 This *Program of Priestly Formation* outlines the requirements shared by diocesan seminarians and by the men in formation for priesthood who are members of an institute of consecrated life or society of apostolic life, while recognizing the different process of formation incumbent both upon those whose primary call is to be of service

85 *Perfectae Caritatis*, no. 2.

to the Church through consecrated life, in a fidelity and witness to the charism of their founder in the gift that is shared,[86] and upon those whose primary call is to be of Christlike service to the Catholic faithful through a commitment in obedience, simplicity of life, celibacy, and holiness.

86 See Sacred Congregation for Religious and for Secular Institutes/Sacred Congregation for Bishops, *Mutuae Relationes* (*Directives for the Mutual Relations Between Bishops and Religious in the Church*, 1978); Congregation for Institutes of Consecrated Life and Societies of Apostolic Life, *Directives on Formation in Religious Institutes* (1990).

Priestly Vocations *in the* Church's Pastoral Work

50 ACCOMPANIMENT OF PRIESTLY VOCATIONS

The whole Church receives and accompanies the gift of vocations from God and is responsible for promoting and discerning vocations.[87] The entire Church is to be engaged in the pastoral work of promoting vocations.[88] It is integral to the mission of the Church "to care for the birth, discernment and fostering of vocations, particularly those to the priesthood."[89] Within that ecclesial context, there are various responsibilities.

a. *The Church*: The whole Church through prayer, active cooperation, and the witness of living full Christian lives takes responsibility for vocations.[90] "Both the family and the parish of origin, or the parish to which he belongs, as well as other ecclesial communities, contribute significantly to sustaining and nourishing the vocation of those called to the priesthood."[91]

b. *The family*: "A very special responsibility falls upon the Christian family, which by virtue of the sacrament of matrimony shares in its own unique way in the educational mission of the Church—teacher and mother." Families can become "'a first seminary' in which children can acquire from the beginning an awareness of piety and prayer and love for the Church."[92]

c. *The parish*: The parish is where vocations are first explored and nourished in the faith and where those who are called come into contact with the clergy, men and women in consecrated life, and lay leaders who accompany them on this journey and encourage them into service. It is vital that the parish develop a culture of vocations to invite youth, young adults, and adults to consider the calls to

87 See *Pastores Dabo Vobis*, nos. 34-41.
88 See CIC, c. 233 §1; CCEO, c. 329.
89 *Pastores Dabo Vobis*, no. 34.
90 See *Pastores Dabo Vobis*, no. 41.
91 *Ratio Fundamentalis*, no. 148.
92 *Pastores Dabo Vobis*, no. 41.

marriage, the priesthood, the permanent diaconate, and consecrated life. Catholic schools and parish religious education programs are supportive environments that foster intellectual curiosity and encourage the development of love of God and neighbor. Rooted in the teachings of the Catholic faith, schools and programs provide an invaluable setting in which vocations to marriage, priesthood, and consecrated life can be nurtured.

d. *The diocesan bishop*: "The first responsibility for the pastoral work of promoting priestly vocations lies with the bishop, who is called to be the first to exercise this responsibility even though he can and must call upon many others to cooperate with him."[93] Although he shares his responsibility, the pastoral task of promoting priestly vocations remains his task, for which he must continue to offer supervision and direct involvement.[94] As the one responsible for the unity of the local Church and its communion with the Universal Church, the bishop, especially in the context of the United States, must encourage a wide range of men who represent the cultural and linguistic diversity of his ecclesiastical entity.

e. *The presbyterate*: "The bishop can rely above all on the cooperation of his presbyterate. All its priests are united to him and share his responsibility in seeking and fostering priestly vocations."[95] They do this by inviting men to consider the priesthood as a possible vocation. For those who are discerning the call, priests can nurture their sense of vocation and be invaluable mentors, accompanying them along the path of discernment. Through their priestly ministry, especially in parish assignments, priests are able to recognize the prayerfulness, the talents, and the character of men who may be called to priestly ministry. "At the same time the diligence of priests in carrying out their Eucharistic ministry, together with the conscious, active and fruitful participation of the faithful in the Eucharist, provides young men with a powerful example and

93 *Pastores Dabo Vobis*, no. 41.
94 See CIC, cc. 233, 385; CCEO, cc. 195, 329 §1, 3°; Congregation for Bishops, *Apostolorum Successores* (*Directory for the Pastoral Ministry of Bishops*, 2004), no. 91.
95 *Pastores Dabo Vobis*, no. 41.

incentive for responding generously to God's call. Often it is the example of a priest's fervent pastoral charity which the Lord uses to sow and to bring to fruition in a young man's heart the seed of a priestly calling."[96]

f. *The vocation director*: In ecclesiastical entities in the United States, generally there is a vocation director (or team) who serves on behalf of the diocesan bishop and presbyterate or of the competent authority to promote vocations (the work of *recruitment*) and to direct those discerning a call to the priesthood.

i. The diocesan vocation director supports, inspires, and equips pastors, parishes, and diocesan personnel to create a culture of vocations in which men can be better equipped to answer God's prompting. Pastors and other members of the community are invaluable in assisting the vocation director in accompanying discerners along the path of discipleship and mission. Once a discerner has been identified, the vocation director works in conjunction with the parish or another community of the faithful to assist in nourishing the seeds of a vocation with divine grace, for example by helping the man to find a spiritual director, maintain an active prayer life, develop a network of relationships with others who bring forth fruits of authentic discernment in one another, and actively seek out a solid participation in the mission of the parish or other community of the faithful. It is important that the vocation director actively develop relationships by his presence, such as regular visits to parishes, youth groups, young adult gatherings, and university campus ministry events.

ii. In cooperating with the formation process, a diocesan vocation director may manage the diocesan process of admission, serve as a liaison between the diocesan bishop and the seminary, and link the seminarian to the diocese and presbyterate, for example, through pastoral placements. He collaborates with the bishop, with the presbyterate, with a diocesan vocation commission if

96 *Ecclesia de Eucharistia*, no. 31.

one is in place, and with the seminary. The role of a vocation director for other ecclesiastical entities may vary according to the division of labor in a given ecclesiastical entity. All vocation directors should collaborate to create a culture of vocations. In all cases, the relationship with the seminary merits special attention. Mutual respect and collaboration should mark the relations between vocation and seminary personnel. Each possesses different responsibilities; yet cooperation, mutual knowledge, and trust are vital for the good of the seminarians and the benefit of the Church. Such collaboration is especially important concerning applicants' ongoing evaluation and their recommendation for admission.

iii. The vocation director accompanies others along their journey, possibly for several years, through their initial discernment, seminary formation, and ordination to the priesthood, if that is the local custom. The vocation director should not attempt to develop a process of formation that competes with or parallels that of the seminary. It is vital that all those responsible for the formation of priests collaborate fully in this work. Regardless of the length of the relationship, the vocation director has a lasting influence on the lives of those he encounters.

g. *National vocations promotion*: Peer organizations such as the National Conference of Diocesan Vocation Directors (NCDVD) and the National Religious Vocation Conference (NRVC) seek to promote vocations to priesthood in various ecclesiastical entities, as well the other various expressions of consecrated life. Each in its own way is a resource to vocations personnel, formators, seminaries, parishes, dioceses, eparchies, personal ordinariates, schools, universities, and those discerning a priestly vocation or a vocation to the various forms of consecrated life. This exchange of ideas, sharing of resources, and development of best practices in promotion, discernment, and formation help those involved in vocational accompaniment. Organizations such as NCDVD and

NRVC help members to build fraternity and support, learn from one another, and serve the discerner and seminarian with the best resources available.

h. *The seminary*: The seminary plays a collaborative role in the promotion of vocations and an important role in the discernment of vocations. A seminary attached to a particular diocese often subsumes the responsibilities of a diocesan vocation director. The seminary community is especially important in promoting, assessing, and developing priestly vocations.

i. *Seminarians*: Seminarians also play a significant role in promoting priestly vocations through the friendships they form outside the seminary setting, through their visible presence in their home parishes, through their involvement in Christian service activities and field education, through their assistance with vocation programs, and through the welcome they extend to visitors at the seminary.

THE DISCERNMENT OF VOCATIONS

51 Discerners for the priesthood must be in prayerful dialogue with God and with the Church in the discernment of their vocation. The linkage of this divine and ecclesial dialogue is especially important because "in the present context there is . . . a certain tendency to view the bond between human beings and God in an individualistic and self-centered way, as if God's call reached the individual by a direct route, without in any way passing through the community."[97] It may be difficult to heed the voice of God in our world of constant distraction.[98] Today's reality makes the role of the vocation director

97 *Pastores Dabo Vobis*, no. 37.

98 "Nowadays listening is becoming more and more difficult, immersed as we are in a society full of noise, overstimulated and bombarded by information. The outer noise that sometimes prevails in our cities and our neighborhoods is often accompanied by our interior dispersion and confusion. This prevents us from pausing and enjoying the taste of contemplation, reflecting serenely on the events of our lives, going about our work with confidence in God's loving plan, and making a fruitful discernment." Pope Francis, Message for the 2018 World Day of Vocations, December 3, 2017, *www.vatican.va/content/francesco/en/messages/vocations/documents/papa-francesco_20171203_55-messaggio-giornata-mondiale-vocazioni.html.*

for any ecclesiastical entity essential in helping someone discern a call to the priesthood.

52 It is important for the vocation director, as much as possible, to enter into dialogue with the discerner and accompany him in this process. Listening is important as well: "Listening, in communication, is an openness of heart which makes possible that closeness without which genuine spiritual encounter cannot occur. Listening helps us to find the right gesture and word which shows that we are more than simply bystanders. Only through such respectful and compassionate listening can we enter on the paths of true growth and awaken a yearning for the Christian ideal: the desire to respond fully to God's love and to bring to fruition what he has sown in our lives."[99] Although he does not serve as a spiritual director for the discerners in his care, the vocation director should have training in sound principles of vocational discernment to be able to assist them in their discernment in the external forum. A joyful witness by the vocation director makes the reality of the priesthood attractive to the one who is called to this vocation. For all discerners, listening and personal accompaniment are critical.

GROWTH IN HISPANIC VOCATIONS

53 As the Church in the United States continues to become increasingly Hispanic, promotion and discernment of vocations in this segment of the Catholic population of the United States is essential, as are vocation promotion and discernment in other populations present in an ecclesiastical entity.[100] At this historical moment, particular attention should be given to US-born Hispanics, who constitute the majority of young people within this population.[101] It may be

99 *Evangelii Gaudium*, no. 171.

100 For more information on culturally diverse populations in the Catholic Church in the United States, see Mark Gray, Mary Gautier, and Thomas Gaunt, SJ, *Cultural Diversity in the Catholic Church in the United States* (Washington, DC: Center for Applied Research in the Apostolate, 2014).

101 See USCCB, *V National Encuentro of Hispanic/Latino Ministry Working Document* (Washington, DC: USCCB, 2018), 150-155.

desirable that a vocation director himself be able to speak Spanish and be well acquainted with specific Hispanic cultures present in his ecclesiastical entity, because vocations recruitment in these cultures often entails building relationships not only with discerners but also with their families. Vocation directors and admission boards must embrace a missionary spirit in their own ecclesiastical entity, with the goal of encountering Hispanics where they are and accompanying them on their discernment journeys. Such commitment sometimes requires offering academic assistance, counseling, and tutoring to help those discerning a priestly call to prepare for formation. Pastoral leaders and communities fostering vocations among Hispanics must be attentive to cultural differences, which will vary greatly across the broad segment of the Hispanic Catholic population in the United States.

HIGH SCHOOL SEMINARIES AND ACCOMPANIMENT OF ADOLESCENTS

54 There are few high school seminaries in the United States. Those that remain should look to the *Ratio Fundamentalis* for guidance in maintaining their formation programs.[102]

102 See *Ratio Fundamentalis*, nos. 16-23.

Admission *into a* Formation Program

55 In contrast to previous generations, when a more homogenous population presented itself for entrance to the seminary, today's applicants represent considerable diversity—not only of personal gifts and levels of maturity but also of significant cultural differences—that must be taken into account. All those involved in the evaluation of applicants for priestly formation must appreciate cultural, generational, educational, and familial differences and be able to recognize which are gifts, which are liabilities, and which are simply indications of a need for further growth.

56 Ultimately, it is the responsibility of the diocesan bishop or major superior of the institute of consecrated life or society of apostolic life to decide whether to admit applicants into priestly formation, in accordance with the criteria which have been properly established.[103] The diocesan bishop or major superior of the institute of consecrated life or society of apostolic life shares his responsibility with the vocation director or vocation team, perhaps also with an admissions board, and with the local parishes. The admissions process requires sacramental records, an autobiography, a review of psychological and medical assessments (with due regard for CIC, c. 220; CCEO, c. 23), interviews, transcripts, criminal background checks, and immigration documentation as well as letters of reference.[104] Diocesan bishops, major superiors, and rectors must have moral conviction about the psychological and physical health of those they admit into priestly formation. In particular, they must be assured that applicants have a requisite level of affective maturity and the capacity to live celibate chastity. They will determine the means necessary to

103 See CIC, c. 241 §1.
104 See CIC, c. 241 §2; CCEO, c. 342 §2; *Charter for the Protection of Children and Young People*, art. 13.

arrive at such certitude, including, for example, their own interviews with applicants, the reliable testimony of those who have known the applicant, and psychological and physical assessments made by expert consultants.

57 Once an applicant is admitted to the propaedeutic stage, the application process contributes to the seminarian's personal plan for priestly formation. Specifically, the observations and conclusions that emerge from the admissions process serve as a significant resource for the seminarian's human, spiritual, intellectual, and pastoral formation. The sharing of this information presumes a due respect for the rights of the seminarian and a strict maintenance of confidentiality. A written consent, signed by the seminarian, is required before any confidential information can be shared.

58 Without denying the importance of evaluating minimal thresholds in all areas of an applicant's development, high standards and strict vigilance are especially necessary in evaluating human thresholds pertaining to sexuality. "*Sexuality* affects all aspects of the human person in the unity of his body and soul. It especially concerns affectivity, the capacity to love and to procreate, and in a more general way the aptitude for forming bonds of communion with others."[105] For the seminary applicant, thresholds pertaining to sexuality serve as the foundation for living a lifelong commitment to healthy, celibate chastity.

59 In forming a prudent judgment about the suitability of an applicant for priestly formation, the principle of gradualism should be used. According to the principle of gradualism, progressively higher levels of expectations should be sought as an individual advances to progressively higher levels of preparation, moving from the

105 *Catechism of the Catholic Church*, no. 2332.

propaedeutic stage into the discipleship, configuration, and vocational synthesis stages. In short, the further a seminarian advances in the program toward priestly ordination, the greater should be his development of the requisite qualities. The principle of gradualism recognizes that it would be unrealistic to expect an applicant for seminary formation who is beginning the propaedeutic stage to be fully mature in all areas. The time devoted to the propaedeutic stage is especially important in determining if the seminarian has the qualities necessary for further priestly formation in the stages that follow.

60 The principle of gradualism, however, does not deny that a minimal level of development is necessary for admission to a priestly formation program. The minimal qualities necessary for admission are properly understood as *thresholds or foundations.* All applicants need to have reached certain thresholds of human, spiritual, intellectual, and pastoral development, which will serve as foundations for further development.

61 Applicants for admission should have attained, at least in some measure appropriate to their chronological age, qualities in those areas represented by the integrated dimensions of formation identified in *Pastores Dabo Vobis*: human, spiritual, intellectual, and pastoral. In trying to determine what is sufficient growth or development in these areas, admission criteria must be clear and specific. For example:

a. Thresholds in the human dimension considered sufficient for admission into the propaedeutic stage mean not only an absence of serious pathology but also a proven capacity to function competently in ordinary human situations without a need for extensive therapeutic or remedial work to be fully functioning, a psychosexual maturity commensurate with chronological age, a genuine empathy that enables the applicant to connect well and personally with others, a demonstrated ability to initiate and sustain friendships, a capacity for growth or conversion, and a deep desire to be a man for others in the likeness of Christ.

b. Sufficient spiritual thresholds include a person who prays regularly, is active in parish life, participates in the Sunday Eucharist and regularly in the Sacrament of Penance, and is drawn to explore and deepen his spiritual life and share it with others. In the case of an applicant for an institute of consecrated life or society of apostolic life, the man should demonstrate a firm acceptance and adherence to the Rule of Life of the institute or the constitution of the society, especially regarding its practices of liturgical, sacramental, and personal prayer.

c. Sufficient intellectual thresholds include proven capacities for critical thinking, an ability to understand both abstract and practical questions, and the capacity to understand other persons and to communicate effectively with them in both oral and written form.

d. Sufficient pastoral thresholds include having a fundamental sense of the Church's mission and a generous willingness and enthusiasm to promote it, having a sensitivity to the needs of others and a desire to respond to them, and having a willingness to initiate action for the good of individuals and communities.

e. Finally, applicants should also have the *right intention* when they present themselves for admission to a priestly formation program. Their intention to pursue preparation for priestly ordination and ministry should correspond to the Church's understanding. Given the probationary nature of the propaedeutic stage to provide a solid basis for the spiritual life and to nurture a greater self-awareness for personal growth—and given that men begin this stage from various backgrounds, levels of maturity, and life experiences—it will take time during the propaedeutic stage for these qualities to be observed and strengthened.

Norms for Admission into a Formation Program

62 Dioceses, along with other ecclesiastical entities, as well as seminaries must have clear written statements of admission policies, including thresholds, which are to be regularly reviewed and updated. These policies include behavioral criteria that place on applicants the burden of qualification for admission to a priestly formation program. In cases of doubt, caution should be taken and the benefit of the doubt given to the Church. It is also important that the seminary admission procedure carefully weigh the potential impact of the admission of each individual on the whole seminary community.

63 A formation program is not the place for long-term therapy or remedial work, which should be completed prior to a decision concerning admission.[106] If during the admission process or during the propaedeutic stage it is determined that long-term or intensive therapy or remedial work is necessary, this work should be completed prior to beginning the propaedeutic stage or the discipleship stage, respectively.

64 Applicants must give evidence of an overall personal balance, good moral character, a love for the truth, and proper motivation. This evidence includes the requisite human, moral, spiritual, intellectual, physical, and psychological qualities for priestly ministry.[107]

65 All applicants should give witness to their conviction that God has brought them to the formation program to discern whether they are really called to the priesthood; and they should commit themselves wholeheartedly to carrying out that discernment, demonstrate dedication to the formation program, and exhibit appropriate respect

---

106 *Guidelines for the Use of Psychology in the Admission and Formation of Candidates for the Priesthood,* no. 8.

107 See CIC, c. 241 §1; CCEO, c. 342 §1. Regarding psychological assessments see *Guidelines for the Use of Psychology in the Admission and Formation of Candidates for the Priesthood*; *Guidelines for the Use of Psychology in Seminary Admissions*; and *Ratio Fundamentalis*, nos. 191-196. Regarding persons with homosexual tendencies, see *Instruction Concerning the Criteria for the Discernment of Vocations with Regard to Persons with Homosexual Tendencies in View of Their Admission to the Seminary and to Holy Orders* (2005) and also *Ratio Fundamentalis*, no. 199. Regarding physical health see *Ratio Fundamentalis*, no. 190.

to their formators. The applicant should be alert both to signs that seem to confirm that call and to counterindications. As the applicant and then seminarian journeys through the stages of formation, there should be a growing sense of confirmation of that call.

66 Applicants must undergo a thorough screening process appropriate to the admission processes. Personal interviews with the applicants, evaluations from their pastors and teachers, records and evaluations from a previous seminary or institute of consecrated life or society of apostolic life if applicable,[108] academic records, standardized test scores, psychological evaluations, and criminal background checks[109] are all components of an effective admission program, and they are weighed together with an assessment of the applicant's motivation. Those who do not fulfill minimal thresholds for admission must not be admitted.

67 It is the responsibility of the vocation director of the ecclesiastical entity to provide the admissions board with a summary of the results of the screening process. It is his responsibility to provide to the rector of the seminary, in a timely and complete fashion, the results of the screening process used by the ecclesiastical entity. Such provision is to be made only with the applicant's previous written consent. In the event that further consultation is needed in a particular case, additional release forms must be obtained.

68 Applicants from diverse ethnic and cultural backgrounds should be given every encouragement. An effort must be made by vocation directors and seminaries to honor every vocational stirring. Propaedeutic programs and seminaries are responsible for ensuring the possession of adequate resources to serve the formative needs of such applicants. Formation requirements should not be lessened, but necessary adaptations may be made to enable admission into the

108 See *Ratio Fundamentalis*, no. 198.
109 See *Charter for the Protection of Children and Young People*, art. 13.

regular course of study. Applicants must have an adequate command of the English language to begin intellectual formation in a seminary in which English is the language of instruction. English-language studies may be undertaken in the seminary before admission into the full, regular courses of seminary study. It is also important that applicants from other countries receive special help in gaining the necessary understanding of the religious and cultural context for priestly ministry and life in the United States.[110]

69 Seminaries and ecclesiastical entities must draw up guidelines for psychologists and admission personnel that describe those human traits and qualities that are consonant with an authentic vocation to the priesthood as well as those counterindications that suggest that the applicant is not suitable for priestly formation. Seminaries as well as ecclesiastical entities must ensure that those who conduct psychological evaluations for them have a sound understanding and acceptance of Christian anthropology and are well versed in and supportive of the Church's expectations for men in priestly formation, especially expectations concerning celibacy, chastity, obedience, and permanence of commitment, as well as the human traits and qualities that are consonant with an authentic priestly vocation.[111]

70 A psychological assessment is an integral part of the admission procedure. Psychological assessments must be administered using methods that do not violate the applicant's right to privacy and confidentiality or do harm to the reputation of the applicant. Further, they "must always be carried out with the previous, explicit, informed and free consent of the candidate."[112] The applicant has an obligation to be honest during the application process regarding

110 For more information on assessment, acceptance, reception, and orientation of international candidates, see *Guidelines for Receiving Pastoral Ministers in the United States*, especially E1-E5; *Guidelines for the Use of Psychology in Seminary Admissions*, 6.

111 See *Guidelines for the Use of Psychology in Seminary Admissions*, 5-7.

112 *Guidelines for the Use of Psychology in the Admission and Formation of Candidates for the Priesthood*, no. 5. See CIC, c. 220; CCEO, c. 23.

any known difficulties of a psychological nature he has experienced as well as any professional counseling he has received.[113] At the same time, the applicant should understand that the testing results will be shared with the diocesan bishop, the vocation director, the rector, and his agent[114] in a way that permits a thorough review. At times formators may need to work with the seminarian on matters related to the evaluation, and thus they will need some knowledge of the assessment. Due care should be observed in correctly interpreting the results of psychological testing in light of the cultural background of applicants.[115] Care must be taken to ensure that psychological records are maintained in a secure manner, respecting the civil laws of the state regarding records retention and divulging of facts contained in the records.[116] In the event that further consultation is needed in a particular case, additional release forms must be obtained.

71 Admission processes should give sufficient attention to the emotional health of applicants. Special care and scrutiny should be given to those who manifest dysfunction or come from dysfunctional families. It is possible for some individuals to address these issues in the course of a formation program through counseling or other means. Their willingness, however, to confront these or other personal issues should be determined prior to the decision about admission. If long-term therapeutic work is indicated, this is best accomplished before the decision is made concerning admission into a priestly formation program. At times, the gravity of family or personal issues is such that, if the discerner has not yet adequately dealt with these issues, entrance into a priestly formation program should be delayed or denied. Similarly, the gravity of family or personal issues is such that, if a seminarian in the propaedeutic stage has not yet adequately dealt

113 See *Ratio Fundamentalis*, no. 193.

114 See *Ratio Fundamentalis*, no. 195.

115 See *Ratio Fundamentalis*, nos. 191-196; *Guidelines for the Use of Psychology in Seminary Admissions*, 3. Regarding linguistic competency and intercultural competency for those conducting psychological testing, see *Guidelines for the Use of Psychology in Seminary Admissions*, 6; *Guidelines for Receiving Pastoral Ministers in the United States*, E1-E2.

116 See *Ratio Fundamentalis*, no. 196; *Guidelines for the Use of Psychology in Seminary Admissions*, 10-11.

with these issues, entrance into the discipleship stage should be delayed or denied.

72 Admission procedures should include an open and frank discussion of the life experiences that applicants bring to the formation program. Their level of insight or self-knowledge and their willingness to address important human issues—such as their interpersonal abilities, evidence of sound peer relationships, their manner of dealing with authority, and their psychosexual development—can be important gauges of their readiness to enter a formation program. If an individual has any significant unresolved human issues, the seminary is well advised to delay admission until greater clarity or resolution is evident. Concerning the capacity to live the charism of celibacy, the applicant is to have lived in continence for a sustained period of time before entering the propaedeutic stage of priestly formation, so that he may give a strong indication to the vocation director and formators of his capacity for continence and self-possession. In discerning the minimal length of this sustained period of time, indicators in the applicant himself—such as age, life experiences, and capacity for growth in psychosexual maturity—should be considered by admissions personnel.

73 Admission procedures should include an evaluation of all internet and social media use, including gaming, by the applicant up to the point of application. It will be necessary for formation personnel to assist the discerner and seminarian with any recommended ongoing support.

74 Any evidence of criminal or compulsive sexual activity or an inclination toward such activity disqualifies the applicant from admission.[117]

117 See *Ratio Fundamentalis*, no. 202. See also *Charter for the Protection of Children and Young People*, art. 13.

75 With regard to the admission of men with same-sex experiences and/or inclinations, the guidelines provided by the Holy See must be followed.[118] To this end a distinction must be made between deep-seated and transitory tendencies. Persons who "practice homosexuality, present deep-seated homosexual tendencies or support the so-called 'gay culture'" cannot be admitted to either the seminary or Holy Orders.[119] "Different, however, would be the case in which one were dealing with homosexual tendencies that were only the expression of a transitory problem—for example, that of an adolescence not yet superseded. Nevertheless, such tendencies must be clearly overcome at least three years before ordination to the diaconate."[120] It is important that formators and, if necessary, outside professionals pastorally accompany a person "in a relationship of sincere dialogue and mutual trust,"[121] especially a discerner or seminarian, as he and the Church discern whether his homosexual tendencies are transitory or deep-seated.

76 Concerning the results of psychological testing and other confidential materials, the ecclesiastical entity and seminary must observe all Canon Law and civil law requirements, inform the applicant in writing of his specific rights to privacy and confidentiality, and utilize appropriate release forms.[122] Throughout the admission process and the priestly formation program, the man's rights to privacy and a good reputation must be respected, and the careful management of confidential materials is to be observed.[123] The wording of any release forms must indicate which persons may have access to the information and with whom they can share it, making it explicit that no other sharing is to be allowed without the man's explicit written

118 See *Instruction Concerning the Criteria for the Discernment of Vocations with Regard to Persons with Homosexual Tendencies in View of Their Admission to the Seminary and to Holy Orders.*

119 *Ratio Fundamentalis*, no. 199.

120 *Ratio Fundamentalis*, no. 200.

121 *Ratio Fundamentalis*, no. 200.

122 See CIC, c. 220; CCEO, c. 23.

123 See *Ratio Fundamentalis*, no. 196. Due to the diversity of state laws, each ecclesiastical entity and seminary is to determine the length of time for which "documentation related to the physical and psychological health of seminarians is to be stored," respecting all applicable civil laws.

permission. In the event that further consultation is needed in a particular case, additional release forms must be obtained.

77 In the initial admission process, an evaluation should be made of an applicant's indebtedness, his ability to handle finances (for example, responsible record keeping and payment of personal taxes), spending patterns, and perhaps a willingness to cover a portion of his formation expenses. Applicants should demonstrate an aptitude for learning principles of good stewardship, avoiding any attitudes of entitlement. They should also show an openness to developing professional approaches to personal and Church-related business matters.

78 The admission process should be attentive to older, experienced applicants, who often bring a mature spirituality, experience in pastoral life, and other significant life experiences but who might also be less docile to formation. The admission processes must be no less rigorous, thorough, or comprehensive than it might be for other applicants.

79 If an applicant has never been in a formation program, then he must complete a propaedeutic stage lasting not less than one calendar year and a discipleship stage lasting not less than a two-year calendar period. Discipleship stage programs that form men with prior life and education experience (bachelor's degree or equivalent) must be designed to address all four dimensions of formation, not simply to meet academic requirements.

80 If applicants have been in a formation program previously, with due regard for what has already been stated regarding criminal or compulsive sexual activity, ecclesiastical entities and seminaries must consult all previous institutions about the past record of these applicants as prescribed in the *Norms Concerning Applications for*

Priestly Formation from Those Previously Enrolled in a Formation Program.[124] While remaining confidential, "the reasons [for dismissal] should be given with the greatest possible objectivity, avoiding ambiguity and the use of euphemisms."[125] It is also important to learn the reasons for leaving, if a seminarian left a formation program on his own initiative. Regardless of whether a seminarian was dismissed or left, if the records indicate difficulties, the ecclesiastical entity and seminary should proceed with due caution and prudence before admitting the applicant and should ascertain whether problems have been resolved and sufficient positive growth has taken place. In serious cases involving issues with Church doctrine or behavior, inside or outside a formation program, admittance is unwise.

81 If an applicant has been dismissed from a program of priestly formation or from an institute of consecrated life or society of apostolic life, no subsequent application will be considered in the two years following such dismissal. If the departure was other than a dismissal, sufficient time should be allotted to evaluate carefully his application and background.

82 Prior to admission into a formation program, the ecclesiastical entity, usually through the vocation director, is obliged to ensure (and the seminary must verify) that recent certificates of Baptism and Confirmation (or Chrismation with holy Myron) have been obtained and to determine (if applicable) into which Eastern Catholic Church *sui iuris* the applicant is ascribed.[126] The diocese must also obtain the following documentation from others: summaries of personal interviews with the applicant, evaluations from his pastor

---

124 See USCCB, *Norms Concerning Reapplication for Priestly Formation*, *www.usccb.org/beliefs-and-teachings/vocations/priesthood/priestly-formation/norms-concerning-reapplication-for-priestly-formation.cfm*; CIC, c. 241 §3; CCEO, c. 342 §3. These *Norms* are to be followed in reviewing an application for enrollment in a program of priestly formation that is submitted by one who has previously been enrolled in such a program or who has belonged to an institute of consecrated life or a society of apostolic life.

125 *Scrutinies*, no. 8.

126 See CIC, c. 241 §2; CCEO, c. 342 §2.

and teachers, academic records, standardized test scores, assessments of the applicant's motivation conducted by experienced formators, and, if applicable, previous seminary evaluations. The seminary must verify the completion of all documentation before an applicant is admitted.

83 The admission process by the ecclesiastical entity also must include a thorough physical examination to ensure that applicants possess the good health necessary for seminary training and priestly ministry. This exam should include HIV and drug testing along with screening that verifies biological maleness.

84 A thorough assessment of an applicant's marital history is a necessary part of the admission process. An applicant for the priesthood in the Latin Church must testify that he is not married, even if only civilly, or that, if he is married, he has received a dispensation from the Apostolic See.[127] If an Eastern Catholic discerner is married, a certificate of marriage is required along with the written consent of his wife[128] and any necessary consultations required by the Apostolic See.[129] Applicants who have received a declaration of matrimonial nullity should be carefully screened. Although these men may have canonical freedom to pursue the priesthood, it is important to ascertain if and how previous obstacles to a marriage commitment or possible scandal might affect their viability as fit applicants for priestly formation. Care must be taken to review the canonical declaration of nullity and the relevant documentation to ensure that the reasons and circumstances that serve as warrants for the declaration of nullity are fully disclosed to the sponsoring bishop or competent authority, rector, and the seminary admissions committee. If a previously married person has natural obligations toward a previous spouse, and/or primary responsibility for a minor child, this information

---

127 See CIC, c. 1047 §2, 3°.
128 See CCEO, c. 769 §1, 2°.
129 See Congregation for the Oriental Churches, *Pontificia Praecepta de Clero Uxorato Orientali*, June 14, 2014, AAS 106: 496-499.

should be carefully considered. All such cases should be carefully weighed.

85 Careful screening should also be given to applicants who are recent converts to the Catholic faith or who have lapsed in the practice of their faith and have recently returned. It is advisable that at least two years pass between their entry into the Church and their admission into the propaedeutic stage. A suitable period of time should pass before entrance into a formation program, in cases of Catholics for whom a sudden conversion experience seems to precipitate a priestly vocation. Similarly, those who return to the practice of the faith after an extended period away from the Church should not enter a formation program directly.

86 The seminary is obligated to determine the freedom of the applicant from the impediments and irregularities for receiving Holy Orders and from conditions that must be addressed prior to the reception of Holy Orders, namely, that sufficient time has passed for a neophyte;[130] that the applicant does not hold a position forbidden to clerics;[131] that the applicant does not "labor under some form of amentia or other psychic illness";[132] that he has not committed the delict of apostasy, heresy, or schism;[133] and that he has not committed voluntary homicide, positively cooperated in a completed abortion,[134] gravely and maliciously mutilated himself or another, attempted suicide,[135] or simulated an act reserved to priests or bishops.[136] If any of these conditions exist, then prior to admission, appropriate dispensations or remedies must be obtained, including, when necessary, recourse to the tribunal of the Apostolic Penitentiary when the existence of the impediment is not a publicly known fact.

130 See CIC, c. 1042, 3°; CCEO, c. 762 §1, 8°.
131 See CIC, cc. 285-286, 289, 1042, 2°; CCEO, cc. 762 §1, 7°, 382-385.
132 See CIC, c. 1041, 1°; CCEO, c. 762 §1, 1°; *Ratio Fundamentalis*, nos. 191-196.
133 See CIC, c. 1041, 2°; CCEO, c. 762 §1, 2°.
134 See CIC, c. 1041, 4°; CCEO, c. 762 §1, 4°.
135 See CIC, c. 1041, 5°; CCEO, c. 762 §1, 5°.
136 See CIC, c. 1041, 6°; CCEO, c. 762 §1, 6°.

87 The diocesan bishop must investigate whether the applicant is allergic to wheat and whether he is able to consume the Precious Blood.[137]

88 The diocesan bishop must investigate whether the applicant has a criminal background.

89 Furthermore, the diocesan bishop must investigate whether the applicant is abusing alcohol or drugs, whether he suffers from an addiction or compulsive disorder to pornography, and whether he is capable of beginning formation.

90 If an applicant has ever been sexually abused, the diocesan bishop or competent authority, with compassionate solicitude for the good of the man and for the good of the Church, must determine whether it is prudent to admit the applicant into a formation program.

137 "Given the centrality of the celebration of the Eucharist in the life of a priest, one must proceed with great caution before admitting to Holy Orders those candidates unable to ingest gluten or alcohol without serious harm." Congregation for the Doctrine of the Faith, *Circular Letter to All Presidents of the Episcopal Conferences Concerning the Use of Low-Gluten Altar Breads and Mustum as Matter for the Celebration of the Eucharist*, July 24, 2003, *www.vatican.va/roman_curia/congregations/cfaith/documents/rc_con_cfaith_doc_20030724_pane-senza-glutine_en.html.*

Seminary Formation: Those *Who* Accompany Seminarians

INTRODUCTION

91 Integral formation is successful when it is supported by a trusting atmosphere of personal and communal accompaniment. "The purpose of personal accompaniment is to carry out vocational discernment and to form the missionary disciple."[138] So too the role of the community is crucial in accompaniment. "Formation comes about every day through interpersonal relationships, moments of exchange and discussion which result in the development of that 'fertile soil,' in which a vocation matures concretely."[139]

92 Relationships characterized by trust are essential for accompaniment to be successful. "The program of formation should explore and outline the concrete ways in which this trust can be encouraged and safeguarded. Above all, those conditions should be sought and fostered, which can, in some way, create a peaceful climate of trust and mutual confidence: fraternity, empathy, understanding, the ability to listen and to share, and especially a coherent witness of life."[140]

93 The relationships in the external forum are those between a seminarian and his bishop or competent authority, including the agents of the bishop or competent authority (rector, vice rector, vocation director, director of seminarians, and other formators, with the exception of the spiritual director). The term "external forum" includes discussions surrounding any observable behavior of the seminarian and the attitudes and motivations related to these behaviors. The Church has a right and responsibility to know the man she is ordaining, and therefore the

138 *Ratio Fundamentalis*, no. 44.
139 *Ratio Fundamentalis*, no. 50.
140 *Ratio Fundamentalis*, no. 47.

seminarian has a corresponding responsibility to let himself be known. These discussions generally include, but are not limited to, vocational discernment, growth in maturity in all four dimensions, integration and behaviors regarding interior freedom, and behaviors related to the promises of prayer, obedience, and celibacy.

94 The primary relationship in the internal forum is that between a seminarian and his spiritual director. The purpose of the "internal forum" is to protect the manifestation of conscience of the seminarian and to provide him the space to share about his interior life with the moral freedom that is necessary for genuine growth and discernment. These discussions generally include, but are not limited to, movements in prayer, vocational discernment, growth in interior freedom, and struggles and growth in preparation for the promises of prayer, obedience, and celibacy.

95 While the manifestation of conscience and sacramental confession are never part of the external forum, over time the seminarian will grow comfortable discussing appropriate interior matters related to his vocation with formators in the external forum. A solid relationship of trust with his formators in both fora will benefit the seminarian as he receives guidance from all formators. This relationship will allow major decisions to be reached following regular discussions throughout the formation process, so that the seminarian will not be surprised by decisions reached by those responsible for his formation, and vice versa. It must be clear that the material of spiritual direction and confession are not to be shared by spiritual directors with external forum personnel.[141]

AGENTS OF FORMATION

96 Accompaniment is the work of the agents of formation. "The principal agent of formation is the Most Holy Trinity, who shapes

141 See Congregation for Catholic Education, *Report on the Apostolic Visitation of the American Seminaries*, December 15, 2008.

every seminarian according to the plan of the Father, both through the presence of Christ in His word, in the sacraments and in the brothers and sisters of the community, and through the many actions of the Holy Spirit."[142] In his docility to the Holy Spirit and the program of initial formation, "each seminarian is the protagonist of his own formation."[143] He is ultimately responsible for his ongoing growth in the human, spiritual, intellectual, and pastoral dimensions of his formation.

THE DIOCESAN BISHOP

97 "It is the Bishop who is primarily responsible for admission to the Seminary and formation for the priesthood."[144] This is expressed in his choice of rector and members of the community of formators, as well as his approval of the seminary Rule of Life. In addition to his administrative responsibilities concerning the seminary, the bishop should "establish a trustful dialogue with seminarians, so as to enable them to be sincere and open."[145] For this to occur, it is important that bishops spend regular time with seminarians, both in one-on-one meetings and in visits to the seminary.[146] The presbyterate, in communion with the diocesan bishop, can serve as companions in helping men to attain formation benchmarks.

THE RECTOR

98 The rector, because of his responsibility for the formation program as a whole, must take an active part in the accompaniment of seminarians. The rector is "to be a priest distinguished by prudence, wisdom and balance, someone highly competent,"[147] who is seen as the father of the entire seminary community. It is the rector who sets the tone for the seminary—a tone which must be characterized by

142 *Ratio Fundamentalis*, no. 125.
143 *Ratio Fundamentalis*, no. 130.
144 *Ratio Fundamentalis*, no. 128.
145 *Ratio Fundamentalis*, no. 128.
146 See CIC, cc. 259 §2, 396-397, 628; CCEO, cc. 205, 356 §2, 420. Similarly, the competent authority of the ecclesiastical entity should foster and promote the vocations of his men preparing for priesthood.
147 *Ratio Fundamentalis*, no. 134.

trust and mutual respect. "With fraternal charity, he will establish a profound and loyal cooperation with the other formators. He is the legal representative of the Seminary, both ecclesiastically and civilly."[148] It is the rector who has daily care for supervision of all aspects of formation in the seminary.[149] He provides regular (at least annual) reports to the diocesan bishop or competent authority of the ecclesiastical entity on the status of each seminarian. Therefore, while other formators, professors, and specialists will assist the rector in his duties, it is important that he know each seminarian personally.

PRIESTLY ACCOMPANIMENT

99 A seminarian must be assigned to an individual priest formator who is in residence in the seminary. This priest is responsible for accompanying the seminarian through that particular stage of formation. This formator accompanies the seminarian in the external forum and is responsible for personalizing the work of seminary formation for an individual seminarian as well as engaging in the discernment process that oversees the suitability of the seminarian for continuation.[150] The formator is at the service of the mystery of vocation in the seminarian. He helps to discern whether such a call is present and to foster it to its fullness by relating to the man as a shepherd and a father.

100 Just as Jesus accompanied his Apostles and offered them individual formation along the way, so also "seminarians need to be accompanied in a personal way in the various stages of their journey by those entrusted with the work of formation."[151] The growth of human formation happens generally in a threefold process of self-knowledge, moving to self-possession, and finally to self-gift, and

148 *Ratio Fundamentalis*, no. 134.
149 See CIC, c. 260.
150 See *Ratio Fundamentalis*, no. 132.
151 *Ratio Fundamentalis*, no. 44.

all this in a context of faith.[152] This is a gradual process of growth that integrates both the human and spiritual life of the man and leads to a deepening of interior freedom. The growth of interior freedom leads ultimately to a configuration to Christ and thus makes him capable and willing to live the Paschal Mystery of Christ in his own life. The formator accompanies the man in this gradual growth process and assists "the seminarian in becoming aware of his condition, of the talents that he has received, and of his frailties, so that he can become ever more receptive to the action of grace."[153] This dialogue will involve challenge and encouragement, correction and accountability, as the formator listens to the deeper motives behind the actions of the seminarian and helps him to integrate the various aspects of his life. It will require cultivating in the seminarian attitudes that promote living a life of virtue. It requires truly knowing the seminarian and his particular growth needs. To this end, "it is important that every seminarian be aware of his own life history, and be ready to share it with his formators. This would include especially his experience of childhood and adolescence, the influence that his family and his relatives have exercised upon him, his ability to establish mature and well balanced interpersonal relationships, or his lack thereof, and his ability to handle positively moments of solitude."[154] Such accompaniment must bring together all the aspects of the human person, allowing him to surrender his whole life to Christ in obedience and interior freedom. "In fact it is only in the crucified and risen Christ that this path of integration finds meaning and completion; all things are united in him (see Eph 1:10)."[155]

101 The key element in this formative accompaniment is mutual trust. It is essential that "the seminarian should know himself and let

152 See USCCB Committee on Priestly Formation, *Spiritual Formation in the Catholic Seminary* (1982).
153 *Ratio Fundamentalis*, no. 46.
154 *Ratio Fundamentalis*, no. 94.
155 *Ratio Fundamentalis*, no. 29.

himself be known."[156] This openness is required for real formation to happen. If a man hides his struggles in formation, growth cannot happen. The seminary community should seek to create the conditions that foster this peaceful climate of trust and mutual confidence through relationships marked by "fraternity, empathy, understanding, the ability to listen and to share, and especially a coherent witness of life."[157] This climate of mutual confidence will be helped by the formators accompanying the seminarians outside of formal meetings in meals, recreation, and other potentially formative experiences. These times can provide excellent opportunities to know the seminarians and provide the formation that comes from witness of life and ordinary encounters. When the seminarian experiences that the priest formators live true fatherhood seeking his good, and that the life of the seminary is marked by a spirit of true fraternity, this trust will not be difficult to establish.[158]

102 To arrive at the necessary depth of formation, conversations between the formator and the seminarian should normally occur about once a month.[159] Just as it is beneficial for seminarians to remain with the same spiritual director for longer periods of time, it is preferable that one formator work with the seminarian in the external forum throughout each particular stage of formation. When possible it is advantageous for a seminarian to have the same formator for even longer than one stage of formation.

103 The Church is clear about the importance of the role of this priest formator and the needed formation for it:

> The formator must exercise discretion when it comes to the lives of seminarians. Each formator should be possessed of human, spiritual, pastoral and professional abilities and resources, so as to provide the

---

156 *Ratio Fundamentalis*, no. 45.
157 *Ratio Fundamentalis*, no. 47.
158 See *Ratio Fundamentalis*, no. 52.
159 See *Ratio Fundamentalis*, no. 46.

right kind of accompaniment that is balanced and respectful of the freedom and the conscience of the other person, and that will help him in his human and spiritual growth. Moreover, those who are marked out to become formators need a specific preparation and generous dedication to this important task. Formators are needed who can ensure their full-time presence and who, above all else, are witnesses of how to love and serve the people of God, giving themselves without reserve for the Church.[160]

The Spiritual Director

104 Seminarians must meet regularly with a priest spiritual director, normally biweekly.[161] Spiritual directors must be chosen freely from a list prepared by the coordinator of spiritual formation. They should have proper training and adequate credentials for the work. These priests must be approved by the rector and appointed by the competent authority.[162] In the case of seminarians for an institute of consecrated life or society of apostolic life, the formation director or competent authority of the institute or society offers guidance on an appropriate spiritual director for the seminarians under his care.

105 Seminarians should confide their personal history, personal relationships, prayer experiences, their cultivation of virtues, their temptations, and other significant topics to their spiritual director. If, for serious reason, there is a change of director, the new director should give attention to continuity in the seminarian's spiritual development.

106 The spiritual director should foster an integration of spiritual formation, human formation, and character development consistent with priestly formation. The spiritual director assists the seminarian in acquiring the skills of spiritual discernment and plays a key role in

160 *Ratio Fundamentalis*, no. 49.
161 See *Ratio Fundamentalis*, no. 107.
162 See CIC, c. 239 §2; CCEO, c. 339 §1.

helping the seminarian discern whether he is called to priesthood or to another vocation in the Church.

107 Those priests who engage in spiritual direction for seminarians must understand and support the full formation program. They also need to be integrated into the priestly community of the seminary. The spiritual directors are thus aware that they are part of the whole seminary program and community.[163]

108 Care is to be taken to ensure that issues of human formation that properly belong to the external forum are not limited to the spiritual direction relationship for their resolution. Likewise, the spiritual director should be prepared to encourage that a seminarian bring to the external forum characteristics within him which would preclude the freedom to be advanced or ordained.

109 Because spiritual direction in a seminary context differs from spiritual direction more generally experienced in the Church, the seminary must explain to seminarians the purpose and process of spiritual direction in the seminary. This should include, for example, an understanding that spiritual direction is not an optional possibility but a seminary requirement; a recognition that seminary spiritual direction is concerned not only with the personal spiritual growth of seminarians but also with their preparation for service in the Church as priests; a knowledge that the spiritual direction process must take into account preparation for ordination and that, therefore, one should have passed certain thresholds of spiritual development and commitment at different points in the seminary program (in contrast to the open-ended nature of nonseminary spiritual direction); and an acceptance that a lack of readiness for spiritual direction itself should

163 See *Ratio Fundamentalis*, nos. 132-133.

prompt a seminarian to question his continuance in the seminary and seriously consider withdrawing from the program until he is ready.[164]

110 Meetings with spiritual directors are to be of sufficient frequency, normally biweekly, and sufficient duration to allow adequate opportunity to assist the seminarian in ongoing vocational discernment, proximate preparation for the reception of ministries and Holy Orders, and formation for celibacy.

111 Disclosures that a seminarian makes in the course of spiritual direction belong to the internal forum. Consequently, the spiritual director is held to the strictest confidentiality concerning information received in spiritual direction. He may neither reveal it nor use it.[165] Although the civil legal requirements might vary from state to state, the only possible exception to this standard of confidentiality would be the case of grave, immediate, or mortal danger involving the directee or another person.[166] If what is revealed in spiritual direction coincides with the celebration of the Sacrament of Penance (in other words, what is revealed is revealed *ad ordinem absolutionis*)—that is, the exchange takes place not only in the nonsacramental internal forum but also in the sacramental internal forum—then the absolute canonical strictures of the seal of confession hold, and no information may be revealed or used.

112 Although the rector may never ask a spiritual director about the content of a seminarian's conversation, he can expect a spiritual director to confirm that a seminarian sees him biweekly. The spiritual director must notify the rector if the director decides to discontinue spiritual direction with any seminarian or if the seminarian discontinues direction with him.

---

164 For example, see *Instruction Concerning the Criteria for the Discernment of Vocations with Regard to Persons with Homosexual Tendencies in View of Their Admission to the Seminary and to Holy Orders.*
165 See CIC, c. 240 §2; CCEO, c. 339 §3.
166 See *Charter for the Protection of Children and Young People*, art. 4.

Lay Accompaniment

113 Although priestly formation necessarily includes agents of formation who must be priests, it is essential that a seminarian's formation be truly ecclesial through the formal participation of lay members of the seminary community. The laity, particularly women, offer insightful recommendations, opinions, and points of view to the rector and community of formators. In addition, families and other communities within the Church are an integral part of the initial stages of formation.

Seminary Formation: Structural Elements

AN INTEGRAL FORMATION

114 Formation, as the Church understands it, is not equivalent to a secular sense of schooling or, even less, of job training. It begins for all Christians at Baptism and continues throughout life. God uses the entirety of one's life experiences continually to invite the believer to draw closer to him. He is always at work in the soul as the master craftsman, shaping and molding us. So too, for those he has chosen to pursue the path of priesthood, whether in a diocesan or a consecrated vocation, his quiet yet constant presence is always at work. "The formation of priests means following a singular 'journey of discipleship,' which begins at Baptism, is perfected through the other sacraments of Christian Initiation, comes to be appreciated as the center of one's life at the beginning of Seminary formation, and continues through the whole of life."[167] While formation is a lifelong journey, the time spent preparing for ordained ministry is a privileged time of growth in self-knowledge and deepening intimacy with Jesus Christ. At the beginning of the seminary journey, "the seminarian is a 'mystery to himself,' in which two aspects of his humanity, that need to be integrated, are intertwined and exist side by side. On the one hand he is characterized by talents and gifts that have been molded by grace; on the other he is marked by his limits and frailty. The task of formation is to help the person to integrate these aspects, under the influence of the Holy Spirit, in a journey of faith and of gradual and harmonious maturity, avoiding fragmentation, polarization, excesses, superficiality or partiality."[168]

167 *Ratio Fundamentalis*, Introduction, no. 3.
168 *Ratio Fundamentalis*, no. 28.

Formation to the priesthood is described in the human, spiritual, intellectual, and pastoral dimensions. However, one must always keep in mind that these dimensions are not compartmentalized but are held in concert with one another. In a similar way, discipleship, configuration, and vocational synthesis, while recognized as stages on the journey toward priesthood, are never finished. Following ordination, the priest always remains a disciple of Jesus Christ, who is called throughout his life to cooperate with God's grace in configuring his life more each day to that of the great High Priest.

115 Integral formation attempts to bring together, as much as possible, the four dimensions of formation in the seminarian as he matures into an authentic priestly identity. The four dimensions of human, spiritual, intellectual, and pastoral formation are interrelated aspects of a human response to God's transforming grace. Without attention to integration in all stages of formation, the overall goal of formation, configuration to the heart and life of the Lord Jesus, cannot be achieved. While each seminary must have a structured plan of formation for all seminarians, the integration of the four dimensions must be personalized in each particular man "to achieve a serene and creative interior synthesis between strength and weakness."[169]

116 Through human formation the foundation is laid upon which the other dimensions can be received and lived. Through spiritual formation, the seminarian learns to bring everything from the other dimensions into his relationship with Jesus Christ. Through intellectual formation he comes to a deeper understanding of the truths of faith and the human person, enriching his relationship with God, his understanding of himself, and his service to others. Through pastoral formation he learns how to express the other three in pastoral charity, the overall goal of priestly formation. It is through

169 *Ratio Fundamentalis*, no. 29.

the integration of all four dimensions that the seminarian comes to the affective maturity and freedom needed for priestly service.

> Each of the dimensions of formation is aimed at "transforming" or "assimilating" the heart in the image of the heart of Christ [cf. *Optatam Totius*, no. 4; *Pastores Dabo Vobis*, no. 57], who was sent by the Father to fulfill his loving plan. He was moved when faced with human suffering (cf. Mt 9:35-36), he went to seek out the lost sheep (cf. Mt 18:12-14), even to offering his life for them (cf. Jn 10:11). He came not to be served but to serve (cf. Mt 20:24-28). As the Second Vatican Council indicates [see *Optatam Totius*, nos. 4, 19], the entire process of formation in preparation for priestly ministry, in fact, has as its aim the preparation of seminarians to "*enter into the communion with the charity of Christ the Good Shepherd.*"[170]

The goal is the development not just of a well-rounded person, a prayerful person, or an experienced pastoral practitioner, but rather of one who understands his formation within the context of his call to service in the Church.

117 In the beginning stages of formation, the seminarian must be presented with specific areas of growth in each dimension so that he is able immediately to see the need for formation within himself, no matter how challenging this may be for him. In the later stages of formation there needs to be a systematic approach to growth in each of the stages of formation with the hopes that the man will naturally see the areas of growth needed in himself and will therefore continue to desire to be formed even after priestly ordination.

SEMINARY STAGES OF FORMATION

118 Formation in the seminary begins by focusing in a concentrated way on the seminarian's relationship with Jesus Christ. The seminarian first became a disciple of Christ at his Baptism; formation in the

170 *Ratio Fundamentalis*, no. 89, quoting *Pastores Dabo Vobis*, no. 57.

seminary will enable him to grow as a disciple who is discerning and preparing for ordained ministry. He is gradually formed into a shepherd who is called to make a gift of his life in pastoral charity for the People of God. This gradual development of the future priest has as its goal growth in holiness, so as to become configured to Christ, Head and Shepherd, Servant and Spouse.

PROPAEDEUTIC STAGE

119 The propaedeutic stage seeks to provide seminarians with the basic groundwork they need to engage in priestly formation. Through no fault of their own, the requisite qualities for formation are often missing in new seminarians. A significant imbalance is present between the lifestyle promoted by contemporary society and priestly formation. There are many generous young men open to a priestly call who nevertheless need more intensive preparation before they are ready to enter into the discipleship stage of formation; thus, a propaedeutic stage prior to the discipleship stage is essential. Indeed, even men who have benefited from stronger formation from family and parish life can still profit from a period of consolidation and growth in prayer, trust, and fraternity. Given that men discern a priestly vocation and apply to a formation program for an ecclesiastical entity from a variety of life circumstances, the propaedeutic stage satisfies the "need to dedicate a period of time to preparation of an introductory nature, in view of the priestly formation to follow or, alternatively, of the decision to follow a different path in life."[171] While the way in which the propaedeutic stage is accomplished in ecclesiastical entities will vary,[172] nonetheless, the stage is mandatory for all men in initial formation.

120 Formation is a lifelong journey. It is important to lay a solid foundation for this journey in the propaedeutic stage, especially in

---

171 *Ratio Fundamentalis*, no. 59.

172 For example, in an institute of consecrated life or society of apostolic life, the propaedeutic stage is accomplished during the postulancy and/or novitiate.

the human and spiritual dimensions, such that the seminarian can thrive in the discipleship, configuration, and vocational synthesis stages of formation. Thus "the propaedeutic stage is an indispensable phase of formation with its own specific character."[173] This stage allows the seminarian to lay a foundation for a new way of life by developing a life of prayer, study, fraternity, and appropriate docility to formation.

121 "In the formation that is offered, emphasis should be placed on communion with one's Bishop, with the presbyterate and with the entire particular Church."[174] Gaining a greater understanding of the local Church and an awareness of the pastoral situations present in one's ecclesiastical entity will assist the seminarian in discerning his vocation. The propaedeutic stage should also offer an opportunity to develop "the dynamic of self-giving through experiences in the parish setting and charitable works."[175]

122 Another central goal of the propaedeutic stage is an intense and profound vocational discernment, undertaken within a community.[176] A first discernment was made during the admission process within the diocese by the bishop, pastor, and vocation director. The propaedeutic stage provides for a second discernment of the seminarian who is living a daily community life for at least twelve months. During this time, it should become clear whether he has the qualities and the maturity to integrate the four dimensions of priestly formation going forward. The propaedeutic stage should conclude with the seminarian's making a firm resolution to dedicate himself to the work of priestly formation or, alternatively, "to follow a different path in life" as a faithful lay Catholic.[177] A decision to proceed to priestly formation must always be confirmed by the Church.

173 *Ratio Fundamentalis*, no. 59.
174 *Ratio Fundamentalis*, no. 60.
175 *Ratio Fundamentalis*, no. 59.
176 See *Ratio Fundamentalis*, no. 60.
177 *Ratio Fundamentalis*, no. 59.

123 Conferences that teach a man how to pray, especially scriptural meditation and the art of *lectio divina*, are essential to the propaedeutic stage. Time for silence, mental prayer, and spiritual reading will help to lay a solid foundation for future stages of formation and ongoing formation. It is encouraged that men in this stage experience retreats that focus on an ability to discern the promptings of the Holy Spirit, an opportunity to develop a strong relationship with Jesus Christ, and vocational discernment.

124 The propaedeutic stage must always be the first of the four stages of initial formation.[178]

125 The propaedeutic stage is "not to be less than one year or more than two";[179] the minimum one-year duration of the propaedeutic stage is twelve calendar months (not an academic year). A third year is permissible provided that the overall character of the stage is preserved throughout. A three-year propaedeutic stage presumes two years of full-time academic studies of a general nature (without philosophical studies, which are restricted to the discipleship stage), followed by one year focused on human, spiritual, and pastoral formation. If this option is utilized, the first two years are not considered part of the discipleship stage, which must not begin until the propaedeutic stage has been completed.

126 The propaedeutic stage should not be confined to times in which a university or college is in session. There might be fewer vacation periods during the propaedeutic stage. For example, while a break may be envisioned for the Christmas holidays, the celebrations of Holy Week and Easter might take place within the propaedeutic community. Further, since this period lasts a full year, a set period at the beginning and again at the end of the propaedeutic stage,

178 See *Ratio Fundamentalis*, no. 59.
179 *Ratio Fundamentalis*, no. 59.

without any courses for academic credit, would assist in ensuring that the goals of this stage are met.

127 "It is fitting that the propaedeutic stage be lived in a community distinct from the Major Seminary and, where at all possible, that it should have its own house."[180] Normally the propaedeutic stage would take place within the ecclesiastical entity, yet it must have an appropriate number of seminarians to support a healthy community. Community life helps the human dimension bear maximum fruit during the propaedeutic stage. These interactions in the normal course of events will contribute to the seminarian's personal plan of formation in this and future stages. The propaedeutic stage must always be lived in a specific community with a team of priest formators. An individualized, "personal" propaedeutic stage, such as an apprenticeship to a pastor living in a rectory, is no substitute, since it cannot fulfill the objectives proper to this stage. If the propaedeutic stage takes place within the ecclesiastical entity, the priests delegated by the competent authority are charged with the responsibility of accompanying the seminarians so that they meet the appropriate benchmarks.

128 The propaedeutic stage may take place in a seminary building as long as it remains distinct from the discipleship and configuration stages. The propaedeutic stage must be truly clear and distinct, with its own formators dedicated to this distinct stage.[181] The *horarium*, scope, and sequence of the propaedeutic stage should be different from the other stages. The propaedeutic stage may have a dress code distinct from that of the discipleship stage, or vice versa. Clerical attire at this stage is premature. Retreats, pilgrimages, and days of reflection may occur more frequently during this stage than in other stages.

---

180 *Ratio Fundamentalis*, no. 60.
181 See *Ratio Fundamentalis*, no. 60.

129 A seminarian can earn college credit for some of his general studies during the propaedeutic stage. Such coursework should not exceed nine credit hours per semester, so that the stage's goals and objectives will be accomplished. Classes proper to the propaedeutic stage's intellectual formation (e.g., biblical literacy, catechesis, prayer and spirituality) must compose the bulk of the intellectual formation of this stage and can be taken for credit.[182] Philosophical studies must not begin until the discipleship stage.

130 Care must be taken that the number of courses does not lay an excessive burden on the man, which could compromise the integrity of the goals and objectives of the propaedeutic stage.

131 The propaedeutic stage allows for flexibility in accord with the principles of the *Ratio Fundamentalis*, adapted to particular needs of seminarians and ecclesiastical entities. The following are options or models to consider.[183]

a. For men entering the seminary with college degrees: the propaedeutic stage should last a minimum of one calendar year followed by a discipleship stage of no less than two years.

b. For men entering the seminary who lack undergraduate degrees, there are three proposed models:

i. First, a propaedeutic stage of one year followed by a discipleship stage of three to four years.

ii. Second, a propaedeutic stage of two years followed by a discipleship stage of two to three years.

iii. Third, a propaedeutic stage of three years followed by a discipleship stage of two to three years. This third model for men entering the seminary who lack undergraduate degrees presumes two years of full-time academic studies of a general nature (without philosophical studies, which are restricted

182 See intellectual formation chapter in this document (nos. 260-364).

183 While a diocesan bishop or major superior may decide initially to observe one of the models indicated, time may reveal that a shift to another of the models would be more beneficial for the seminarian as well as the seminary.

to the discipleship stage), followed by one year focused on human, spiritual, and pastoral formation.

Discipleship Stage

132 In the discipleship stage, which must not last less than two years,[184] there is a systematic and rigorous formation that has at its core the goal of growing in an intimate relationship with Jesus Christ through the life of meditation and contemplation,[185] as well as the training of one's character in Christian virtue, so as to lay a solid foundation for future stages. The study of philosophy occurs during the discipleship stage.

133 Men enter the discipleship stage at varying levels of life, work, and educational experience. Initial formation programs for the discipleship stage should be designed to take these circumstances into account. There are programs designed to meet the needs of young men who have recently completed high school and who may have minimal work and education experience. Other priestly formation programs or variants of programs can be developed to meet the needs of older men who come to the discipleship stage with life, work, and educational experience.[186]

134 The seminarian intensely discerns his vocation to the priesthood during the discipleship stage, and thus he can clearly articulate his call and his conviction to be a priest. Having received positive confirmation from formators, the seminarian is advanced into the configuration stage, at which time candidacy is received.[187]

---

184 See *Ratio Fundamentalis*, no. 66.

185 *Optatam Totius*, no. 8, describes the careful development of spiritual training so that "the students might learn to live in intimate and unceasing union with God the Father through his Son Jesus Christ, in the Holy Spirit."

186 In the past these programs have been referred to as pretheology programs. The term "pretheology" with its inference of academic status is discouraged because it can obscure the integral nature of formation in the discipleship stage. Nevertheless, these men are a distinctive set of seminarians who come to initial formation with more extensive experiences on many levels; a formation program should take these unique circumstances into account.

187 See *Ratio Fundamentalis*, no. 67.

CONFIGURATION STAGE

135 In the configuration stage, the seminarian models his life on the self-donation of Jesus Christ, Shepherd and Servant, as he prepares more immediately for Holy Orders. "This configuration demands that the seminarian enter profoundly into the contemplation of the person of Jesus Christ, the beloved Son of the Father, sent as Shepherd of the People of God. It will make the relationship with Christ more intimate and personal and, at the same time, will lead to an awareness and an assumption of priestly identity."[188] Formation in priestly spirituality involves a heartfelt dedication to his ecclesiastical entity in loving obedience.

136 The configuration stage demands from the seminarian a great commitment, as it challenges him to acquire a proper priestly spirituality; this includes a greater awareness and personal assumption of priestly identity as he conforms himself to the sentiments and attitudes of the Son, understood as self-offering for the pastoral care of the sheep. Conferral of the ministries of lector and acolyte is appropriate during this stage, marking the progressive deepening of this self-configuration to Christ both liturgically and in catechesis, evangelization, and active service to the poor.[189]

VOCATIONAL SYNTHESIS STAGE

137 The vocational synthesis stage begins upon the completion of the configuration stage. It is intended primarily as a time not of evaluation, but of integration and transition. Based on the principle of gradualism as found in the *Ratio Fundamentalis*, the vocational synthesis stage is a gradual realization of the cleric's responsibility for the care of souls while he resides full-time in a pastoral setting, usually the parish. The goal of the vocational synthesis stage is to

188 *Ratio Fundamentalis*, no. 68.

189 See *Ratio Fundamentalis*, no. 72; CIC, c. 230 §1; USCCB, "Complementary Norms, Canon 230, §1 - Installed Lay Ministries," (2000).

help the deacon make this essential transition before assuming the full responsibilities of priestly life and ministry in the context of his particular ecclesiastical entity. Thus, the vocational synthesis stage is distinct from what is commonly referred to as a "pastoral year."[190]

138 The purpose of the vocational synthesis stage is to allow a deacon to enter into the life of a cleric, incorporating the entirety of the formation he has received from the moment of Baptism until his reception of Holy Orders. Rather than "on-the-job training," this stage is the living of a vocation as an ordained minister, because the diaconate is a new ontological and existential reality. The vocational synthesis stage is not a period of discernment for the priesthood, which began intensely in the propaedeutic stage and was confirmed during the discipleship and configuration stages. The goal is not so much acquiring new pastoral skills—though these certainly will be gained—but more adjusting well to the life of ministry before advancing to priestly ordination. It is about the deacon's readiness to assume the duties of full-time priestly ministry. Therefore, it is not a question of suitability for Holy Orders, which was judged during the scrutiny prior to diaconate ordination, but a preparation for the final judgment regarding the conferral of the Order of Priesthood which should be made upon the completion of the vocational synthesis stage.[191]

139 The vocational synthesis stage takes place "outside the Seminary building"[192] and "is the time from leaving the Seminary until the subsequent priestly ordination, which obviously is brought about by the conferral of the diaconate."[193] The vocational synthesis stage takes place within the ecclesiastical entity which the deacon is preparing to serve, since by diaconal ordination the cleric is incardinated into the

190 See CIC, c. 1032 §2.
191 See CIC, cc. 1028, 1030.
192 *Ratio Fundamentalis*, no. 75.
193 *Ratio Fundamentalis*, no. 74.

particular local Church, institute, or society. Thus, another purpose of this stage is the integration of the deacon into the clergy of his diocese, institute, or society, a process that should precede his entrance into the Order of Priests. In this way, the vocation of the deacon is consolidated within a concrete reality, within his own ecclesiastical entity, accompanied by his bishop, superior, presbyterate, religious community, and parish. This provides for a particular formation which most seminaries cannot offer. While every seminary should be capable of forming men to become priests, most seminaries cannot form men to be priests of their own particular ecclesiastical entity.

140 During this stage, the primary formator of the newly ordained cleric is the pastor of the parish where the deacon is assigned, or the bishop or major superior may delegate another priest of the diocese, institute, or society to fulfill this task. The pastor—who should be an exemplary model of the priesthood,[194] aware of his formative task and of his duty to accompany the transitional deacon—should ensure that there are opportunities for discussion of pastoral situations and opportunities for priestly fraternity that will help the deacon transition well to active ministry and ongoing formation.

141 In this way, the deacon may experience the life of clerical ministry in an environment of openness and dialogue with the pastor, who should accompany him personally and directly regarding his ministerial experiences. This would be accomplished through fraternal and formal exchanges between the deacon and the pastor, such that the preparedness of the deacon for entrance into full priestly life can be evaluated. The trust which has been established and strengthened throughout his years of seminary formation allows him to trust his brothers in ordained ministry, the pastoral team responsible for guiding and evaluating him, and above all his diocesan bishop or the

194 See *Ratio Fundamentalis*, nos. 75, 77.

competent authority of his institute of consecrated life or society of apostolic life, whose decisions he accepts with docility.

142 The formation of the deacon in this stage is essentially different from the formation he received in the seminary, in that it involves the accompaniment of the newly ordained cleric to appreciate his new status in the Church as an official representative and a public figure: incorporating, again, all of the human, spiritual, intellectual, and pastoral formation he has received preceding his entrance into the clerical state. In the vocational synthesis stage, the deacon focuses directly on the needs of the people he is called to serve. He applies what he has learned to pastoral situations and recognizes where he needs and desires ongoing growth. The deacon also seeks to become more integrated into the presbyterate and local Church to which he belongs or in which his institute of consecrated life or society of apostolic life is located.

143 Though the vocational synthesis stage takes place outside the seminary, in some dioceses it may be desirable that deacons be accompanied by formators from the seminary. For example, the deacons could gather at the seminary monthly, once every two months, or quarterly for days of prayer, group reflection, and fraternity in order to process the experience of diaconal ministry and engage in sacramental and pastoral *practica.* Whatever role the seminary may play, a substantial majority of the deacon's time should be spent engaged in ministry in his diocese, institute, or society. Virtual technology could also be used by the seminary to assist in this accompaniment.

144 The minimum duration of the vocational synthesis stage is six months of residence and diaconal ministry in the diocese, institute, or society.

145 This stage always takes place after the completion of the configuration stage (i.e., the stages are never concurrent). A seminarian petitions for diaconate ordination at the conclusion of the configuration stage or during the vocational synthesis stage.[195]

146 Because the mission of the diaconate is oriented toward ministry, rather than academic study, it would be optimal for the seminarian to complete the equivalent of four years of theological studies before petitioning to receive diaconal ordination.[196] Having completed all of his academic requirements, a man can peacefully turn his attention toward diaconal and priestly ministry.

147 With the foregoing in mind, the following are three flexible models regarding the vocational synthesis stage that meet the requirements of the *Ratio Fundamentalis* and are adapted to the realities of priestly formation in the United States.

a. *Model A.* Configuration stage lasting four years: diaconate ordination upon successful completion of the configuration stage (including four full years of theological studies), and vocational synthesis stage lasting at least six months in a parish after leaving the seminary).[197]

b. *Model B.* Configuration stage lasting three and three-quarters years: diaconate ordination upon successful completion of the configuration stage, and vocational synthesis stage lasting one to three months in the seminary (to complete the four years of theological studies) and then at least six months in a parish after leaving the seminary.

195 See *Ratio Fundamentalis*, no. 73. Although CIC, c. 1032 §1, says that "those aspiring to the presbyterate can be promoted to the diaconate only after they have completed the fifth year of the curriculum of philosophical and theological studies," it does not mandate this practice; CIC specifies the minimum amount of time prior to diaconate ordination. The *Ratio Fundamentalis* specifies that a man may not petition for orders until the completion of the configuration stage.

196 See *Ratio Fundamentalis*, no. 73.

197 See CIC, c. 1031 §1.

c. *Model C.* Configuration stage lasting three and one-half years: diaconate ordination upon successful completion of the configuration stage and the equivalent of four years of theological studies, and vocational synthesis stage lasting at least six months in a parish after leaving the seminary.[198]

148 After an initial decision to observe one of the models indicated above for the vocational synthesis stage, time may reveal that a shift to another of the models would be more beneficial for an individual deacon or a particular diocese.

COMMUNITY

149 Priestly formation occurs in the context of a community, whether a seminary or a house of formation. It is "a continuation in the Church of the apostolic community gathered about Jesus" in which men called to share in a unique way in the priesthood of Christ relive today the formation offered to the Twelve by the Lord.[199] What follows also applies to religious seminarians *mutatis mutandis.*

150 The seminary's life in community mirrors ecclesial communion, which itself is rooted in the Blessed Trinity. This ecclesiology of communion lived out in seminary community is "decisive for understanding the identity of the priest, his essential dignity, and his vocation and mission among the People of God and in the world."[200] Viewed in this way, the seminary community is the essential formational matrix for those preparing for ordained ministry, which itself "has a radical 'communitarian form' and can only be carried out as a 'collective work.'"[201] The seminary community, then, is committed to fostering

198 In this last model, it could be possible for a candidate to take what is equivalent to four years of theological studies, eight semesters, in three and one-half years, possibly using summer sessions. It must be kept in mind that an exaggerated emphasis on the intellectual dimension should not restrict growth in the other three dimensions of formation.

199 See *Pastores Dabo Vobis*, nos. 60-61.

200 *Pastores Dabo Vobis*, no. 12.

201 *Pastores Dabo Vobis*, no. 17.

the human, spiritual, intellectual, and pastoral formation of future priests.[202]

151 The essential work of the seminary takes place in the context of community. Personal growth and character development should progress together harmoniously within a deepening spiritual life. Community life can help overcome difficulties caused by excessive individualism. "Formation comes about every day through interpersonal relationships, moments of exchange and discussion which result in the development of that 'fertile soil,' in which a vocation matures concretely."[203] The seminary is a school of human virtue and of growth in honesty, integrity, intellectual rigor, hard work, and tolerance, where the common good is built with solidarity and discipline—all leavened by humor and healthy enjoyment. The seminary is also a school of spiritual growth in which seminarians are formed into men of prayer, imbued with those virtues that only grace can bring: faith, hope, and charity. "In fact, fraternity is fostered through spiritual growth, which requires a constant effort to overcome various forms of individualism. A fraternal relationship 'cannot just be left to chance, to fortuitous circumstances,' but is rather a conscious choice and an ongoing challenge."[204] The seminary helps the seminarians develop the relationship and dialogue skills necessary for healthy interpersonal relationships as priests.

152 Seminary programs of formation have two focal points: (1) the seminary community and its public life as an environment for growth and development that includes many different kinds of relationships, and (2) individual seminarians as they strive to interiorize the values of the spiritual life and integrate the lessons of human, spiritual,

202 See *Pastores Dabo Vobis*, no. 61.
203 *Ratio Fundamentalis*, no. 50.
204 *Ratio Fundamentalis*, no. 52. See also Pope Francis, "Meeting with Diocesan Priests in the Cathedral of Cassano all'Jonio" (June 21, 2014), *L'Osservatore Romano* 140 (June 22, 2014): 7.

intellectual, and pastoral formation. The interplay between individual and community, founded on Christ, lies at the heart of formation.

153 The experience of the seminary community plays a significant role in the personal and spiritual growth of seminarians. Each stage of formation will shape community in a particular way. Still, at every stage, community is formative in similar ways. The give-and-take among those who share the priesthood as a common vocation sets the right context for formation. Such interaction provides mutual support, promotes tolerance and fraternal correction, and gives an opportunity for the development of leadership and talent among seminarians. It also can motivate seminarians to develop a sense of self-sacrifice and a spirit of collaboration.[205] The seminarians and the community of formators form the heart of the seminary community, and this reality needs careful cultivation so that the distinctive aims of seminary formation can be achieved.

Norms for Community

154 Seminarians are to be fully committed to the life of the seminary community and are to learn how to contribute generously to it and to receive humbly from its resources.

155 With an eye toward the exercise of future pastoral responsibilities, seminarians should give evidence of an ability to follow a schedule with community prayer at its heart, allowing time for a healthy balance of personal prayer, study, enjoyment of the arts, physical exercise, leisure, and social interaction; seminarians should develop discerning habits in reading, the use of various media, the internet, and entertainment in general.[206]

205 "Seminarians are bound, both individually and as a group, to demonstrate—and not only in their external behavior—that they have internalized an authentically priestly way of life, in humility and in service of their brothers. This is a sign of a mature choice to give themselves to following Christ in a special way." *Ratio Fundamentalis*, no. 131.

206 See *Ratio Fundamentalis*, nos. 99-100.

156 Each seminary must have a handbook based on the *Program of Priestly Formation*, approved by the diocesan bishop or major superior, in which the expectations of the formation program of the seminary are clearly stated. These expectations specify the human, spiritual, intellectual, and pastoral components of that formation program and include a Rule of Life as mandated by the *Code of Canon Law* and the *Code of Canons of the Eastern Churches.*[207] The handbook forms the basis of an annual evaluation of the seminarians and is regularly reviewed and updated. In addition to a Rule of Life, the handbook also includes the seminary's statutes, mission statement, policies and procedures, criteria for admission and ongoing evaluation, process of evaluation, appropriate calendars and schedules, and a description of seminary community roles and house jobs.

157 A Rule of Life—approved by the diocesan bishop or, in the case of an interdiocesan seminary, the bishops involved—is necessary to regulate day-to-day living and to articulate the common values that give a community integrity and purpose. The Rule adapts the *Program of Priestly Formation* to particular circumstances and especially determines more precisely the points of discipline that pertain to daily life of seminarians and the order of the community. A Rule of Life addresses the essentials of community living while avoiding excessive detail that would stifle individual initiative or talent. It also seeks to balance freedom, responsibility, accountability, activities, and solitude.

158 The rector's conferences are especially helpful in aiding seminarians to interpret rightly their life in common, their discernment of vocation to the priesthood, and the human and spiritual virtues they strive to appropriate.

---

207 See CIC, c. 243; CCEO, c. 337 §§2-3.

159 The expectations and procedures of the evaluation process must be detailed in the handbook and explained clearly to the seminary community by the rector or his delegate each year.

160 Matters pertaining to celibate and chaste living must be included in the seminary Rule of Life. This Rule should also "cultivate the spirit of poverty in practical ways. . . . through simplicity and austerity of life,"[208] encouraging fasting, almsgiving, and the asceticism demanded by a Christian life and the priestly state. In imitating Christ who "became poor although he was rich" (2 Cor 8:9), the seminarian is able to grow in freedom and is able to develop in his heart a special place for the poor and the weak. The seminary environment itself should foster a simple way of life and a spirit of forthright detachment. Seminarians should be made aware that they are accountable for the proper stewardship of material goods and personal health. The Rule of Life must encourage appropriate respect for those in authority and a mature sense of obedience.

161 The seminary should create a climate for mutual respect, communication, and collaboration as a contribution to the overall development of the seminarians as they interact with many other individuals and communities as well. Men and women mingle with seminarians in a variety of settings: personal, academic, pastoral, and ecumenical. The interaction of seminarians with seminary administrative staff and service personnel in the seminary community often reveals attitudes toward others in general. Seminarians' ongoing contact with their own family and parish or ecclesial movement should continue to form a significant dimension of their life. "The community forms the seedbed of a priestly vocation, since the seminarian emerges from it, in order to be sent back to serve it after ordination. The seminarian to begin with, and later the priest, must have a living bond with the

208 *Ratio Fundamentalis*, no. 111.

community."[209] Seminarians should participate in parish activities and volunteer for service on a regular basis.

162 The seminary community and individual seminarians should appreciate the presence of a multicultural, multiethnic, and international community within the seminary. This environment provides a mutually enriching dimension to a seminary community and reflects the realities of pastoral life awaiting seminarians. This diversity should also help seminarians develop a quality of adaptability to varied pastoral settings in their future priestly ministry.

THE CONTINUING EVALUATION OF SEMINARIANS

163 The continuing evaluation of seminarians is linked to their formation as well as to the Church's responsibility to discern vocations to priesthood as a gift from God. Since formation assumes that a seminarian will be growing both in God's grace and in his free, human response to that grace, it is important that there be a process to note the benchmarks of that growth. In this way, the Church provides seminarians with encouragement to continue their formation and also with wisdom to identify ways in which that formation may take deeper root. The Church's responsibility to discern the authenticity of vocations also implies some process whereby the Church, usually working through the seminary, scrutinizes the seminarian's aptness and readiness to assume the responsibilities of ordained ministry. This ongoing evaluation of seminarians, then, affirms, strengthens, and fosters growth in formation while continuing the process of discernment.

Norms for the Continuing Evaluation of Seminarians

164 The seminary is responsible for the continuing evaluation of seminarians regarding their progress in priestly formation. The process

209 *Ratio Fundamentalis*, no. 90. The bonds between formators and seminarians and among the seminarians themselves are also important and "must be marked by a sense of fatherhood and fraternity." *Ratio Fundamentalis*, no. 52.

of evaluation must be clearly described in detail in the seminary handbook. The seminary should have a written statement of the criteria used in evaluating seminarians. Such evaluation is primarily the responsibility of the rector and the community of formators. It should also involve the input of the seminarians themselves, their various supervisors, and their peers.

165 Each seminary must provide a procedure for the evaluation of seminarians. As part of this procedure, each seminary should ensure that seminarians are apprised of their progress as early as possible in their formation, particularly if there are concerns; that the priest formator regularly communicates with the seminarians; that the seminarians have a procedure for responding to matters raised in the evaluation process; that confidentiality, as articulated by the seminary, is observed; and that all doubts are resolved in favor of the Church.[210] The process of evaluation should be conducted in an atmosphere of mutual trust and confidence. It should promote the continued growth of the seminarian in the four dimensions of formation. Each seminarian should be evaluated on the basis of his actual progress and maturation, not on the basis of the mere passage of time.[211]

166 Seminarians are accountable for all aspects of priestly formation within the four dimensions of human, spiritual, intellectual, and pastoral formation. This accountability includes participation in spiritual exercises, the spiritual direction program, liturgical exercises, and community life as well as the intellectual and pastoral dimensions of priestly formation. This approach is taken because all the aspects of priestly formation are "intimately interwoven and should not be

---

210 The unity of the good must always be remembered; that is, the good of the Church can never contradict the good of the individual but always implicitly includes it.

211 See *Ratio Fundamentalis*, no. 58.

separated from one another."[212] "The concept of integral formation is of the greatest importance, since it is the whole person, with all that he is and all that he possesses, who will be at the Lord's service in the Christian community."[213]

167 A seminarian's self-evaluation can be a valuable instrument. Seminarians should prepare such evaluations with an honest and candid examination of themselves in the areas of human, spiritual, intellectual, and pastoral formation. They should recognize their strengths and weaknesses, their positive qualities as well as their areas of needed growth. It is the responsibility of the seminarian to show positive qualities that recommend his advancement in formation. This self-evaluation is done best in consultation with a priest formator.

168 Peer evaluations are recommended as helpful in the evaluation process. Such evaluations must be conducted in a responsible and confidential manner. Seminarians completing peer evaluations should be exhorted to do so with honesty and in a spirit of charity. Positive or negative opinions concerning the suitability of a peer for advancement should be expressed clearly.

169 The seminary should require an evaluation of a seminarian's pastoral activities from his appropriate supervisor. This report should give attention to all dimensions of formation.

170 The evaluative process culminates in a yearly written report from the rector to the diocesan bishop or major superior that provides a clear estimation of the seminarian's progress in the areas of human, spiritual, intellectual, and pastoral formation.[214] The annual report

---

212 Association of Theological Schools (ATS), The Commission of Accrediting, *General Institutional Standards*, 3.1.1.
213 *Ratio Fundamentalis*, no. 92.
214 See *Ratio Fundamentalis*, no. 204.

should include the results of the vote of the community of formators regarding the seminarian's advancement, supplying the number of affirmative and negative votes as well as the number of abstentions. Both negative votes and abstentions should be explained.

171 The annual evaluation should include a well-founded judgment concerning the suitability of the seminarian for advancement to the next year or stage of formation. The evaluation report should be detailed. The qualities listed in Canon Law for promotion to Holy Orders are considered at each stage of advancement: integral faith, right intention, requisite knowledge, good reputation, integral morals and proven virtues, and the requisite physical and psychological health.[215] The evaluation should provide a judgment of the seminarian's aptitude for priestly life and ministry as well as an estimation of his capacity to lead a chaste, celibate life. The seminarian's current stage in formation should be considered in assessing his readiness for advancement. The individual benchmarks pertaining to each stage of formation are presented for each dimension of formation in the chapters that follow. These are to be considered and applied, according to the principle of gradualism, at each stage of formation.

172 The content of the annual evaluation must be communicated to each seminarian with a signed acknowledgment of having reviewed the evaluation. A written copy may be given to him.

173 The annual evaluation may be concurrent with the scrutiny required for each liturgical ritual that marks the seminarian's advancement toward the priesthood, providing clear indications regarding his suitability.[216] The norms of the Church are to be observed regarding admission to candidacy and institution into the ministries of lector

215 See CIC, c. 1029; CCEO, c. 758.
216 See *Scrutinies*.

and acolyte (Latin Church)[217] or lower orders (Eastern Catholic Churches).[218] The proper documentation must be collected for the scrutiny for each stage. The procedures and documentation required prior to ordination to the diaconate and to the priesthood are to be completed.[219]

174 Seminarians must have exercised the ministries of lector and acolyte (Latin Church) or lower orders (Eastern Catholic Churches) for a suitable period of time before ordination to the diaconate (CIC, c. 1035 §1; CCEO, c. 758 §1, 5°). There is to be an interval of at least six months between the conferral of the ministry of acolyte (Latin Church) and ordination to the diaconate (CIC, c. 1035 §2). Prior to ordination to the diaconate, the candidate is to make a canonical retreat (CIC, c. 1039; CCEO, c. 772), take the Oath of Fidelity,[220] and make the Profession of Faith (CIC, c. 833, 6°). The candidate is to be at least twenty-three years of age (CIC, c. 1031 §1; CCEO, c. 759). He is to have completed at least five years of philosophy and theology (CIC, c. 1032 §1; CCEO, c. 760); is to have received candidacy, except for vowed members of clerical institutes (CIC, c. 1034); is to be able to articulate the theology and expectations of the diaconate (CIC, c. 1028); and in writing is to petition his diocesan bishop or major superior to be ordained, expressing his free intention and permanent commitment (CIC, cc. 1034 §1, 1036; CCEO, c. 761). The seminary is to certify to the diocesan bishop or major superior that all these requirements have been met (CIC, c. 1050, 1°; CCEO, c. 769, §1 1°). The rector verifies that the candidate for the diaconate accepts the teachings of the Church, prays the complete Liturgy of the Hours (or the Divine Praises, for the Eastern Catholic Churches), attends daily Mass, receives the Sacrament of Penance regularly, and is committed to a life of celibacy.

---

217 See CIC, cc. 1034-1035; St. Paul VI, apostolic letters given *Motu Proprio*: *Ministeria Quaedam* and *Ad Pascendum* (August 15, 1972).

218 See CCEO, c. 758 §1, 5°.

219 See CIC, cc. 1050-1052; CCEO, cc. 769-770.

220 See *Acta Apostolicae Sedis* (AAS) 81 (1989): 104-106.

175 A judgment concerning the suitability of a candidate to receive the diaconate as a transitional step to priesthood includes a judgment concerning his suitability for priestly ministry. It is not possible to admit a candidate to the diaconate in the face of doubts concerning his suitability for the priesthood. For this reason the judgment reached by the scrutiny undertaken with a view to ordination to the diaconate is decisive. If this judgment is positive, it should be changed only in the light of new and grave information in the course of the next scrutiny prior to priestly ordination.[221]

176 Deacons must exercise the diaconal order for a suitable period of time before being ordained to the priesthood (CIC, c. 1032 §2). This vocational synthesis stage "has a twofold purpose: on the one hand it is about being inducted into the pastoral life, with a gradual assumption of responsibilities in a spirit of service; on the other hand it is about making a suitable preparation, with the help of a specific accompaniment, in view of priesthood."[222] There is to be an interval of at least six months between a seminarian's ordination to the diaconate and his ordination to the priesthood (CIC, c. 1031 §1). He is to be at least twenty-five years of age and possess sufficient maturity (CIC, c. 1031 §1; CCEO, c. 759 §1). He is to have completed six years of philosophy and theology (CIC, c. 1032 §2; CCEO, c. 760 §2) and is to be able to articulate the theology and expectations of the priesthood (CIC, c. 1028). He is to petition his diocesan bishop or major superior in writing to be ordained, expressing his free intention and permanent commitment (CIC, c. 1036; CCEO, c. 761). The vocation director, the pastor of the parish where the deacon is assigned, or the bishop's or religious superior's delegated priest formator is to certify to the diocesan bishop or major superior that all these requirements have been met (CIC, c. 1050, 1°; CCEO, c. 769, 3°). The vocation director, the pastor of the parish where the deacon is assigned, or the bishop's or religious superior's delegated

221 See *Scrutinies*, no. 11.
222 *Ratio Fundamentalis*, no. 74.

priest formator verifies that the candidate for the priesthood is ready to assume the teaching, sanctifying, and governing mission of Christ. Furthermore, he should demonstrate pastoral love for others and faithful obedience, in conformity with Christ.[223] Prior to ordination to the priesthood, the candidate is to make a canonical retreat (CIC, c. 1039; CCEO, c. 772) and take the Oath of Fidelity.[224]

177 The final judgment about a seminarian's admission to candidacy (or perpetual profession, for members of institutes of consecrated life or societies of apostolic life), institution into the ministries of lector and acolyte, and ordination to the diaconate and priesthood belongs to the diocesan bishop or major superior. He must issue his official call in the name of the Church on the basis of a moral certitude that is founded upon positive evidence proving the suitability of a candidate for Holy Orders (CIC, cc. 1052 §1, 1025 §§1-2, and 1029; CCEO, c. 770). The seminary's evaluations are important in providing this evidence. If such positive evidence is lacking, the seminary must not recommend the advancement of a seminarian.[225]

178 Seminarians who lack the positive qualities for continuing in formation should not be advanced in the seminary program. They should be advised to leave the seminary. In these cases an opportunity should be provided for the seminarian to present his self-assessment, including the possibility of others who can speak on his behalf.

---

223 The diocesan bishop or competent superior may make use of a formation commission, consisting, for example, of the vocation director, the vicar for clergy, other priests, religious, and laity. This commission could provide discernment regarding readiness for priestly ordination at the conclusion of the vocational synthesis stage. The commission should ordinarily proceed by consensus, but the final recommendation to the diocesan bishop or religious superior belongs to the vocation director.

224 See *Scrutinies*, Enclosure IV.

225 Regarding moral certitude, "the fundamental principle in this matter consists in the fact that the competent authority must issue the official call in the name of the Church on the basis of a moral certitude that is founded upon positive reasons regarding the suitability of the candidate (c. 1052, §1, with c. 1025, §§1-2, and c. 1029)." Further, "Although the call [to Holy Orders] is a canonical act which pertains to a personal authority it is clear that such an authority ought not proceed merely on the basis of his convictions or intuitions, but should give a hearing to the opinion of persons and councils and not depart from these except on the strength of well-founded reasons (c. 127, §2, 2°)." *Scrutinies*, nos. 2-3.

Seminarians not recommended for advancement should be notified as early as possible and in a constructive manner.

179 When there is doubt about the readiness of a seminarian for advancement, consideration can be given to a recommendation of a period of probation outside the seminary. The time period involved should be specified, not open-ended. The period of probation should have clearly identified goals and means to assess the achievement of goals. Likewise, appropriate supervision is necessary so that this period away from the seminary might bring about needed growth for the seminarian's possible return to the seminary. If doubts remain after this period, the seminarian should not continue in formation.

180 Houses of formation should maintain appropriate collaborative relationships with the administration and professors of universities and colleges to aid in the evaluation of their seminarians.

Human Dimension

181 The foundation and center of all human formation is the Word made flesh. In his fully developed humanity, he was truly free and with complete freedom gave himself totally for the salvation of the world.[226] *Pastores Dabo Vobis* expresses the Christological foundation of human formation: "The Letter to the Hebrews clearly affirms the 'human character' of God's minister": "he comes from the human community and is at its service, imitating Jesus Christ 'who in every respect has been tempted as we are, yet without sin' (Heb 4:15)."[227]

182 The basic principle of human formation is found in *Pastores Dabo Vobis*: the human personality of the priest is to be a bridge and not an obstacle for others in their meeting with Jesus Christ, the Redeemer of the human race. As the humanity of the Word made flesh was the *instrumentum salutis*, so the humanity of the priest is instrumental in mediating the redemptive gifts of Christ to people today.[228] The disciple of Jesus Christ is a person who is free *to be* who he is in God's design: someone who does not—in contrast to the popular culture—conceive or pursue freedom as the expansion of options or as individual autonomy detached from others, but who rather overcomes every form of self-promotion or emotional dependency.[229] So that the seminarian might act with interior freedom rather than simply demonstrating a "veneer of virtuous habits," human formation seeks to help the seminarian grow in interior maturity.[230] As *Pastores Dabo Vobis* emphasizes, human formation is the "necessary foundation" of priestly formation.[231]

---

226 See Jn 10:17-18; Mk 10:45.

227 *Pastores Dabo Vobis*, no. 5.

228 From this foundation would stem those particular human qualities identified by St. John Paul II in *Pastores Dabo Vobis*, no. 43: "These qualities are needed for them to be balanced people, strong and free, capable of bearing the weight of pastoral responsibilities. They need to be educated to love the truth, to be loyal, to respect every person, to have a sense of justice, to be true to their word, to be genuinely compassionate, to be men of integrity and, especially, to be balanced in judgment and behavior."

229 See *Veritatis Splendor*, no. 34.

230 *Ratio Fundamentalis*, no. 41.

231 *Pastores Dabo Vobis*, no. 43.

183 The human formation of men for the priesthood aims to prepare them to be apt instruments of Christ's grace. It does so by fostering the growth of a man who can be described in these ways:

a. *A person of solid moral character with a finely developed moral conscience, a man open to and capable of conversion*: A man who demonstrates the human virtues of prudence, justice, fortitude, temperance, humility, chastity, constancy, sincerity, patience, good manners, truthfulness, and keeping his word, and who also manifests growth in the practice of these virtues.

b. *A prudent and discerning man*: Someone who demonstrates a "capacity for critical observation" so that he "can discern true and false values, since this is an essential requirement for establishing a constructive dialogue with the world of today."[232]

c. *A man of communion*: A person who has real and deep relational capacities, someone who can enter into genuine dialogue and friendship, a person of true empathy who can understand and know other persons, a person open to others and available to them with a generosity of spirit. The man of communion is capable of making a gift of himself and of receiving the gift of others. This ability, in fact, requires the full possession of himself. This life should be one of inner joy and inner peace—signs of self-possession and generosity.

d. *A good communicator*: Someone who listens well, is articulate, and has the skills of effective communication and public speaking.

e. *A person of affective maturity*: Someone whose life of feelings is in balance and integrated into thought and values; in other words, a man of feelings who is not driven by them but who freely lives his life enriched by them. This might be especially evident in his ability to live well with authority, in his ability to take direction from another, and in his ability to exercise authority well among his peers, as well as an ability to deal productively with conflict and stress.

232 *Ecclesia in America*, no. 40.

f. *A man who demonstrates growth in respect for, care of, and vigilance over his body*: A person who pays appropriate attention to his physical well-being (including weight, exercise, consumption of food and drink, and hygiene), so that he has the energy and strength to accomplish the tasks entrusted to him and the self-knowledge to face temptation and resist it effectively.

g. *A man who relates well with others, free of prejudice, and who is willing to work with people of diverse cultural backgrounds*: A man capable of wholesome relations with women and men[233] as relatives, friends, colleagues, staff members, and teachers and as people encountered in areas of apostolic work.

h. *A good steward of material possessions*: Someone who is able to live a simple style of life and to "refrain from all things that have a semblance of vanity";[234] someone who has the right attitude toward the goods of this world, since his portion and inheritance is the Lord;[235] someone who is generous in making charitable contributions and sustaining the poor.[236]

i. *A man who can take on the role of a public person*: Someone both secure in himself and convinced of his responsibility, who is able to live not just as a private citizen but as a public person in service of the Gospel and representing the Church.

184 Education in the awareness and mature use of social media is a vital component of human formation in seminaries. Prudence and discernment are more important in our current environment than they perhaps were in the past because information technology in our era advances exponentially faster than at any other time in human history. On the one hand, information technology can be used as a powerful tool for pastoral ministry, most notably evangelization. On the other hand, it habituates us to substituting the virtual for the

233 See *Ratio Fundamentalis*, no. 95.
234 CIC, c. 282 §1; CCEO, c. 385 §1.
235 See Ps 16:5-6.
236 See *Presbyterorum Ordinis*, no. 17; CIC, c. 282 §2; CCEO, c. 385 §1.

real, desensitizing us to reality. In addition, careless and undiscerning use of information technology is morally dangerous and may lead to addictive behavior. Seminarians must be taught "how to use these technologies in a competent and appropriate way, shaped by sound theological insights and reflecting a strong priestly spirituality grounded in constant dialogue with the Lord."[237] Seminarians must use social media and technology in accordance with local diocesan/eparchial policies, especially in regard to communication with minors.

185 Human formation comes together in a particular way in the domain of human sexuality, and this is especially true for those who are preparing for a life of celibacy. The various dimensions of being a human person—the physical, the psychological, and the spiritual—converge in affective maturity, which includes human sexuality. Education is necessary for understanding sexuality and living chastely. Those preparing to live out a celibate commitment face particular challenges, especially in today's cultural context of permissiveness and easy access to pornography.

186 Education for chastity, a virtue incumbent on all Christians and in a unique way embraced in celibacy, presents it as a "virtue that develops a person's authentic maturity and makes him or her capable of respecting and fostering the 'nuptial meaning' of the body."[238] For all Christians, whatever their state of life, chastity cultivates the capacity for authentic self-gift in generative and faithful love. The celibate person renounces the realization of this capacity in marriage but embraces it in a universalizing love extended to all people. At the same time, the celibate commitment requires the development of particular habits and skills of living and relating in order to live the commitment with integrity. "Since the charism of celibacy,

237 *Ratio Fundamentalis*, no. 97; see *Ratio Fundamentalis*, nos. 97-100.
238 *Pastores Dabo Vobis*, no. 44.

even when it is genuine and has proved itself, leaves one's affections and instinctive impulses intact, candidates to the priesthood need an affective maturity which is prudent, able to renounce anything that is a threat to it, vigilant over both body and spirit, and capable of esteem and respect in interpersonal relationships between men and women."[239]

187 Seminary formation in sexuality and celibacy communicates to men in priestly formation and enables them to appropriate the following:

a. Their call to priestly celibacy as a share in the chastity of Christ, Head and Shepherd, Servant and Spouse[240]

b. The physiological and psychological understanding of human sexuality

c. The meaning of the virtue of chastity, which includes a formation in authentic principles of sexual maturity and chastity, including virginity,[241] and which also includes "a proper knowledge of the duties and dignity of Christian marriage, which represents the love which exists between Christ and the Church"[242]

d. The requisite skills for living chastely: ascetical practice, prudent self-mastery, and paths of self-knowledge, such as a regular personal inventory and the examination of conscience

e. The meaning of celibate chastity, especially the theological rationale that makes clear how it pertains to the logic of the ordained priesthood

f. The means to live celibate chastity well, including genuine friendships; priestly fraternity; a mentoring relationship; spiritual direction; priestly asceticism, which honestly reckons with the sacrifices that celibacy entails; and especially the Sacrament of Penance

---

239 *Pastores Dabo Vobis*, no. 44.

240 See *Sacramentum Caritatis*, no. 24.

241 See Congregation for Catholic Education, *Training for Priestly Celibacy* (1993), and Sacred Congregation for Catholic Education, *A Guide to Formation in Priestly Celibacy* (1974), 46.

242 *Optatam Totius*, no. 10.

g. The ability to form mature, chaste relationships with both "men and women of various ages and social conditions," both in his personal life and in pastoral ministry[243]

h. The spiritual path that transforms the experience of loneliness into a holy solitude based on a "strong, lively and personal love for Jesus Christ"[244]

i. An attitude that discerns the culture in the light of the Gospel,[245] seeing the positive and negative potentials of mass communications, various forms of entertainment, and technology, such as the internet[246]

j. The capacity—for seminarians who are married or are discerning marriage in those jurisdictions that permit the priestly ordination of married men—to "shine forth with the splendor of chastity" and "to offer an outstanding example to other Christian faithful" in conducting family life and in educating children[247]

188 In general, human formation happens in a threefold process of self-knowledge, self-possession, and self-gift—and all of this in faith.[248] As this process unfolds, the human person becomes more perfectly conformed to the perfect humanity of Jesus Christ, the Word made flesh.[249] The resources for fostering this process of human formation in a seminary context are many. They include the following:

a. *Instruction*: The rector and other members of the seminary community offer the seminarians instruction in human formation through conferences, courses, and other educational means.

b. *Personal reflection*: Seminarians are trained to live life reflectively and to examine, with regularity, their behavior, their

243 *Ratio Fundamentalis*, no. 95.
244 *Pastores Dabo Vobis*, no. 44.
245 See *Gaudium et Spes*, no. 4.
246 See CIC, c. 666.
247 CCEO, cc. 374 and 375.
248 See USCCB Committee on Priestly Formation, *Spiritual Formation in the Catholic Seminary* (1982).
249 See Sacred Congregation for Catholic Education, *A Guide to Formation in Priestly Celibacy* (1974), 19.

motivations, their inclinations, and in general their appropriation of life experience, especially suffering.

c. *Community life and feedback*: "A seminarian who freely chooses to enter a seminary must also freely accept and respect its terms."[250] The general demands and the rewards of life in community expand self-knowledge and self-control and cultivate generosity of spirit. The community's attachment to Sacred Scripture and the sacramental life provides a reflective mirror that helps individuals know themselves and summons them to a fuller, more human, more spiritual life. A community's Rule of Life fosters discipline, self-mastery, and faithful perseverance in commitments.

d. *Application to the tasks of seminary life*: Human formation develops through interaction with others in the course of the seminary program. This growth happens, for example, when seminarians learn to accept the authority of superiors, develop the habit of "using their freedom with discretion," learn to act on their own initiative and to do so energetically, and learn to work "harmoniously with their confreres and with the laity."[251]

e. *Psychological counseling*: On occasion, consultation with a psychologist or other licensed mental health professional can be a useful instrument of human formation. Some patterns of behavior, for example, which became set in the seminarian's early family history, may impede his relational abilities. Understanding one's psychological history and developing strategies to address elements of negative impact can be very helpful in human formation. This kind of counseling or consultation is distinguished from extensive psychotherapy, which may be needed to address deeply entrenched personal issues that impede full functioning of the person. The seminarian already completed psychological testing as part of the application process. At that time, if extensive and in-depth therapy was necessary, it took place outside of the seminary context prior

250 Sacred Congregation for Catholic Education, *A Guide to Formation in Priestly Celibacy* (1974), 74.
251 *Optatam Totius*, no. 11.

to the decision concerning admission. It can also be the case that the necessity for such extensive therapy emerges after admission. In the latter case the seminarian is to withdraw from the program and pursue the therapy before being considered for readmission to the seminary and resuming his advancement to Holy Orders.

Those who provide these psychological services may not be voting members of the formation team in discerning the admission, continuance, or ordination of a man.[252] Normally, any in-depth assessment regarding the admission or continuance of a man in formation should be made by an outside mental health professional to avoid dual relationships. If the psychologist or other representative of the psychological sciences is a member of the seminary community, their roles are confined to training, teaching, and consulting for therapeutic issues that do not involve serious psychopathology. There should be a very clear agreement of understanding that limits the role and boundaries of such persons in seminary formation, under the purview of the rector. A psychologist might be offered for a seminarian who is asked to explore some issue in formation. Voluntary appointments initiated by seminarians with a psychologist must include a clear discussion of the limits of confidentiality and the need to integrate—implicitly or explicitly—the work of counseling with the priest formator and/or spiritual director.

189 It is advisable for each seminary to develop "benchmarks of human formation" and to identify them clearly for the seminary community and seminarians.[253]

190 It is both possible and necessary to integrate human formation with the other three dimensions of formation—the spiritual, the intellectual, and the pastoral. Human formation is integrated with spiritual formation by the Incarnate Word and by the fact that grace builds

252 See *Ratio Fundamentalis*, no. 192.

253 The benchmarks for the initial stages of formation are presented for each dimension in this document and may be useful for seminaries in developing this list.

on nature and perfects nature. Human formation is integrated with intellectual formation by the cultivation of the human functions of perception, analysis, and judgment. It also contributes to intellectual formation by enabling seminarians to pursue theology as a response to the questions of the human condition. Human formation is integrated with pastoral formation, which enables a priest to connect with and care for others with his human personality. Conversely, pastoral formation sharpens his human skills and empathic capacities.

PROPAEDEUTIC STAGE BENCHMARKS

191 Self-knowledge and awareness are key themes in the area of human formation during the propaedeutic stage. Before he begins the discipleship stage, it is important that the seminarian, with the help of formators, be able to reflect upon his personal history (e.g., family of origin, use of technology, personal habits) and his needed areas of growth. Other aspects of the human dimension necessary for beginning the discipleship stage include relational skills (e.g., capacity for healthy and deep friendships, basic social skills and good manners, flexibility, adaptability, a basic capacity for empathy); self-discipline (e.g., capacity for hard work, awareness of the appropriate use of time, basic self-control); a trusting relationship with formators (e.g., openness to correction, awareness of the importance of transparency in formation, growing sense of accountability); and healthy habits of self-care (e.g., beginning an exercise regimen, good personal hygiene, beginning to address any health concerns or unhealthy habits).

DISCIPLESHIP STAGE BENCHMARKS

192 The discipleship stage places special emphasis on human formation[254] and on the necessity of self-awareness and pastoral correction on behalf of the seminarian's formators for continued growth in affective maturity. It is a period marked by the understanding of

254 See *Ratio Fundamentalis*, nos. 62-63.

and growth in the human virtues, informed and perfected by charity. "This process of formation is intended to educate the person in the truth of his being, in freedom and in self-control. It is meant to overcome all kinds of individualism, and to foster the sincere gift of self, opening him to generous dedication to others."[255]

193 During the discipleship stage, the seminarian continues to learn how to integrate his own self-awareness into a desire to grow in affective maturity as he relates to others in the seminary community. Self-awareness can lead to self-acceptance, self-possession, and eventually to self-gift, as seen in his relational skills.

194 In addition to demonstrating appropriate boundaries, by the end of this stage he will have the ability to self-reflect on and communicate appropriately emotions surrounding conflict and stress; he exhibits deepening friendships with other seminarians and manifests growth in the virtues of prudence, justice, fortitude, and temperance. He demonstrates growth in the admirable human qualities of humility, chastity, constancy, sincerity, patience, good manners, truthfulness, keeping his word, gratitude, affability, liberality, meekness, magnanimity, and perseverance. He exhibits racial sensitivity in his words and actions.

195 Regarding self-discipline, he develops the tools to manage stress and maintain balance in his life, as well as the ability to use freedom with prudence and discretion. He has greater awareness of the dynamics of his family of origin, and he shares that knowledge appropriately. He exhibits growing transparency with his formators, an openness to formation, and accountability regarding seminary expectations.

---

255 *Ratio Fundamentalis*, no. 63.

196 The Church needs and deserves healthy priests. By the completion of the discipleship stage, the seminarian demonstrates discipline with his personal and communal *horarium* (e.g., having a regular bedtime and being on time to events) and is developing an exercise regimen or participating in some form of communal exercise. He has demonstrated growth in addressing any health concerns, such as unhealthy weight or unhealthy habits.[256] By the end of the discipleship stage, the seminarian is able to regulate his personal use of social media, gaming, and the internet, and he understands and practices healthy alternatives to the overuse of media.

197 By the end of the discipleship stage, the seminarian will determine with firm resolve whether God is calling him to present himself for the priesthood. His transition to the configuration stage is marked by a level of self-knowledge that permits ongoing growth, especially in his relationships with others. God's grace will then build upon a human nature that is more mature.

CONFIGURATION STAGE BENCHMARKS

198 The seminarian shows evidence of affective maturity in his ability to take direction from another in a healthy manner, especially from those in authority; he also exercises authority and leadership well among his peers. He demonstrates that he deals appropriately with conflict and stress. The completion of the configuration stage is marked by continued growth in interiority and communion; in other words, he demonstrates interior freedom, self-possession, self-motivation, direction, and the capacity for self-donation. The seminarian has internalized seminary expectations and is an example for younger seminarians. He demonstrates this, for example, in his willingness to volunteer for additional responsibilities in the seminary and in

256 Some examples of unhealthy habits are the poor use of time; excessive engagement with social media, gaming, television, or other forms of entertainment; and lack of discipline regarding monetary spending habits.

his avoidance of gossip and cynicism. The seminarian's life in the community should reveal his ability for selfless leadership and the relational qualities of solidarity, compassion, empathy, and attentive listening. Continued growth in self-discipline means that he can plan and follow through on assignments, academic and pastoral; that he sets appropriate priorities in his schedule and resolves scheduling conflicts; and that he possesses a strong work ethic.

199 The seminarian further consolidates the healthy habits of self-care in the configuration stage that he began in the discipleship stage. By the end of the configuration stage, he can be described as a man who cares for, respects, and has vigilance over his body. He exhibits continued growth in addressing any health concerns, and he demonstrates balanced habits of exercise and rest. He has also developed a workable strategy for handling psychological issues in his life. As part of his overall health and well-being, he has well-established habits regarding the proper use of technology (meaning that he limits the entertainment uses of technology and demonstrates appropriate accountability with peers and formators regarding his use of technology). Also, through evaluations, apostolic work, and community living, the seminarian demonstrates an awareness of and capacity to manage appropriate boundaries.[257]

VOCATIONAL SYNTHESIS STAGE BENCHMARKS

200 The personality of the transitional deacon is to be a bridge, not an obstacle, to pastoral ministry, such that he can relate to and accompany the many diverse peoples living in various states of life and different cultures. During this stage he works to overcome any human fears, and he grows in the freedom of natural self-confidence to be able to bring the Gospel to all those who need it.[258] To that end, during

257 In formulating criteria for evaluating candidates, seminaries will find the 1997 *Scrutinies* from the Congregation for Divine Worship and the Discipline of the Sacraments an invaluable and authoritative resource.

258 See *Ratio Fundamentalis*, no. 119.

this stage it is evident that he is capable of having and invested in maintaining wholesome friendships with priests and others and that he willingly participates in presbyteral gatherings. He is committed to mentoring relationships with men and women who assist in his pastoral placement. He demonstrates appropriate transparency in his relationships with his supervisor and staff and is accountable to them regarding his responsibilities and schedule. Being a healthy member of a presbyterate also includes the ability to initiate and spend time with priests and people from diverse generations, ethnicities, and viewpoints; it demonstrates the ability to live the communal nature of the priesthood.

201 As the transitional deacon transitions to full-time ministry, it is important that he shows the ability to maintain regular habits of prayer, rest, exercise, and study and that he exercises good stewardship in a rectory or other communal setting. Having already established healthy habits and strategies of addressing any ongoing health concerns, in this stage he identifies (if necessary) and completes visits to long-term health care professionals (e.g., physician, dentist, and so on). He recognizes the need for and demonstrates ongoing vigilance regarding the use of technology, and he exhibits appropriate accountability with peers and his supervisor regarding the use of technology.

Norms for Human Formation

Aim of the Human Formation Program

202 Every seminary must have a program of human formation appropriate to each stage of formation, which seeks to prepare men to be bridges for, not obstacles to, the spread of the Gospel. The identity to be fostered in the seminarian is that he becomes a man of communion, that is, someone who makes a gift of himself and is able to receive the gift of others.[259] He needs integrity and self-possession in order

259 See *Ratio Fundamentalis*, nos. 41, 52.

to make such a gift. The capacity to be fostered is the affective ability to engage in pastoral leadership with Jesus as the model Shepherd.[260]

203 This program must have a clear focus on the ordained priesthood as a vocation that brings the seminarians to full human and spiritual potential through love of God and service of others. Through conferences offered by the rector and others and through other formation activities, as well as by the theology taught in the academic program, the seminary should make explicit the Church's doctrinal understanding of the ministerial priesthood on which its programs are based.

The Goals of Human Formation

204 The qualities to be fostered in a human formation program are freedom, openness, honesty, flexibility, empathy, joy and inner peace, generosity and justice, chastity, personal maturity, interpersonal skills, common sense, aptitude for ministry, and growth "in moral integrity and public witness."[261] Following St. Thomas Aquinas, human formation should be understood as education in the human virtues perfected by charity.

205 Seminarians should give evidence of having interiorized their seminary formation. Growth in self-awareness and a sound personal identity are the hallmarks of a healthy personality that establishes a secure basis for the spiritual life. Such growth may be demonstrated by sound prudential judgment, a sense of responsibility and personal initiative, a capacity for courageous and decisive leadership, an ability to establish and maintain wholesome friendships, and an ability to work in a collaborative, professional manner with women

260 See ATS, *Degree Program Standards*, A 2.4.2. See CCEO, c. 346 §2, 8°: "Let them also esteem and cultivate those virtues that are most valued by people and commend the minister of Christ, among which are sincerity, a keen concern for justice, a spirit of poverty, fidelity to one's promises, good manners, modesty in conversation joined with charity."

261 ATS, *Degree Program Standards*, A 2.4.

and men, foregoing self-interests in favor of cooperative effort for the common good.

The Seminarian in Human Formation

206 Seminarians bear the primary responsibility for their human formation. The role of the seminary is to assist them in achieving the integral human maturity.

207 The seminarian's human formation is very much affected by the character formation he has received in his family, cultural background, and society. Just as the seminary recognizes that the positive qualities of a seminarian's prior formation can both indicate a vocation and provide a solid foundation for further growth, it should also address possible deficiencies in his earlier formation and find means to address them.

208 Human formation programs in the seminary should begin with the assumption that the seminarians have the potential to move from self-preoccupation to an openness to transcendent values and a concern for the welfare of others. Seminarians should have a history of sound and rewarding peer relationships, an ability to be honest with themselves and with others, and an ability to trust the Church and the agents of formation. Formation programs will not be effective for those who manifest extreme inflexibility, narcissism, antisocial behavior or any serious personality disorders or pathology,[262] a lack of sexual integration, deep and unresolved anger (especially against authority), a deep attachment to a materialist lifestyle, or compulsive behaviors or addictions.

Preparation for Celibate Chastity

209 Preparation for celibacy is one of the primary aims of the human formation program of any seminary. The seminary must have a

262 See *Ratio Fundamentalis*, no. 191.

coordinated and multifaceted program of instruction, prayerful discernment, dialogue, and encouragement that will aid seminarians to understand the nature and purpose of celibate chastity and to embrace it wholeheartedly in their lives. Sexuality finds its authentic meaning in relation to mature love. Seminarians should understand and manifest a mature love as preparation for a celibate life. The insights of modern psychology can be a considerable aid. The goal of psychosexual, social, and spiritual development should be to form seminarians into chaste, celibate men who are loving pastors of the people they serve.[263]

210 The rector should hold periodic conferences on this topic, at least on a yearly basis, in which basic attitudinal and behavioral expectations about the practice of celibacy for priests and seminarians are detailed. He should clearly delineate the kinds of attitudes and behaviors that are acceptable and praiseworthy and the kinds that are not, including an awareness of appropriate boundaries. The rector should address the responsibilities of individual seminarians, both now and later, for themselves and for the common reputation of the community and the priesthood. Clear, concrete terms must be used about the actual meaning of the celibate commitment in the seminary community and later in priestly ministry, if presentations about the value of celibacy are to be persuasive or taken seriously.

211 Human formation for celibacy should aim toward an affective maturity, which is the ability to live a true and responsible love. Signs of affective maturity in the seminarian are prudence, vigilance over body and spirit, compassion and care for others, an ability to express and acknowledge emotions, and a capacity to esteem and respect interpersonal relationships between men and women. Therefore, true friendship is an education in affective maturity.

---

263 See *Pastores Dabo Vobis*, no. 44.

212 To live fully an effective life of celibate chastity, in imitation of Christ's sacrificial love, requires knowledge of one's own sexuality and rightly ordered sexual desires.[264] Certain habits or skills are necessary instruments on the path to healthy celibate chastity, and these are to be encouraged in seminary programs. Among these habits and skills are appropriate self-disclosure, a cultivated capacity for self-reflection, an ability to enter into peaceful solitude, ascetical practices that foster vigilance and self-mastery over one's impulses and drives, and a habit of modesty. An especially important practice is holding all persons in the mystery of God, whether they are encountered in the course of formal ministry or ordinary life. This practice means viewing all persons in God, interceding for them before God, and claiming responsibility to direct them to God.

213 A seminary human formation program should inculcate additional skills for celibate living as care for others, a deepening of the capacity to give and receive love, an ability to practice appropriate self-disclosure, an ability to develop and maintain healthy and inclusive peer friendships, and an ability to set appropriate boundaries by choosing not to act on romantic feelings and by developing self-discipline in the face of temptation. A seminarian must be prepared to accept wholeheartedly the Church's teaching on sexuality in its entirety, be determined to master all sexual temptations, be prepared to meet the challenge of living chastely in all friendships, and finally be resolved to fashion his sexual desires and passions in such a way that he is able to live a healthy, celibate lifestyle that expresses self-gift in faithful and life-giving love: being attentive to others, helping them reach their potential, not giving up, and investing all one's energies in the service of the Kingdom of God. Given the pervasive reality of pornography in today's culture, each program is to address

264 A rightly ordered sexual desire is ordered toward a monogamous, exclusive marriage between a man and woman for the procreation of children.

this problem, as well as the appropriate use of electronic media, with pertinent policies and training in virtue.[265]

214 The seminary must have written guidelines for admission, evaluation, and community life that spell out its expectations regarding those attitudes, behaviors, and levels of psychosexual maturity that indicate a right mentality, proper motivation, and a commitment to celibate chastity. These guidelines should also specify unacceptable attitudes and behaviors that run counter to such a commitment.

215 Any seminarian found to have pathological sexual attraction to minors is to be dismissed from the seminary with no possibility for readmission to the same or another seminary.[266]

Preparation for Simplicity of Life

216 Human formation should cultivate a spirit of generosity, encouraging the seminarian to become a man for others and to curb expectations of entitlement; seminarians should learn practical ways of living simplicity of life.[267] Manifestations of undue materialism and consumerism in the seminarian's behavior should be confronted and corrected.

217 The formation program should articulate the distinctive qualities of simplicity of life appropriate for one preparing for priestly leadership. Simplicity of life is particularly important in our own age when human needs and desires are so consciously manipulated and exploited. A consumer society often reduces people to things, which are used and then discarded, plunging society more deeply into a

265 See USCCB, *Create in Me a Clean Heart: A Pastoral Response to Pornography* (Washington, DC: USCCB, 2015).

266 See *Ratio Fundamentalis*, no. 191.

267 "A right attitude to the world and to earthly goods . . . is of great importance for priests for this reason, that the Church's mission is carried out in the midst of the world and that created goods are absolutely necessary for man's personal progress. Let priests be thankful then for everything that the heavenly Father has given them towards a proper standard of living. However, they ought to judge everything they meet in the light of faith, so that they will be guided towards the right use of things in accordance with God's will and will reject anything that is prejudicial to their mission." *Presbyterorum Ordinis*, no. 17.

world of objects, which ironically seem to possess us. In a consumer society, a right attitude toward the world and earthly goods is easily lost. That is why a seminarian has to be helped to cultivate personal self-discipline and asceticism. It is an important pastoral obligation of all priests who accompany people through the journey of life to acquire a sound and balanced perspective about earthly goods and possessions so that they can impart right attitudes to others.[268]

218 The seminary should foster simplicity of life. Such an attitude does not disparage the world but sees it in light of freedom and service. Priests are able to understand correctly "that the Church's mission is carried out in the midst of the world and that created goods are absolutely necessary for man's personal progress."[269] They can also better appreciate that when the passion for acquisition and possession is curbed, the human capacity for appreciation and enjoyment of the world often is enhanced.

Preparation for Obedience

219 The seminary should articulate appropriate behaviors that manifest a healthy understanding of obedience. The exercise of authority and the response of obedience are works of grace, goodwill, and human effort that play a part in the life of every priest. Seminarians should appreciate and integrate the necessary role that authority and organization play in achieving and maintaining any community's goals and purposes, as well as recognize the theological and spiritual dimension of reverence and obedience in the Catholic Church. Belief with divine and Catholic faith is owed to Divine Revelation, as given by God and proposed by the Church.[270] Doctrine concerning faith or morals, proposed definitively by the Holy Father or the college

268 "Already being used to sacrificing willingly and generously what is not needed, they . . . [can] become sincere and credible promoters of true social justice." *Ratio Fundamentalis*, no. 111.

269 *Presbyterorum Ordinis*, no. 17.

270 See CIC, c. 750 §1; CCEO, c. 598 §1; St. John Paul II, *Ad Tuendam Fidem* (1990).

of bishops, is to be firmly embraced and retained.[271] Additionally, religious submission of the intellect and will is due to doctrine declared by the Holy Father or the college of bishops concerning faith and morals, even if they do not intend to proclaim it definitively.[272] Every bishop is an authentic teacher and instructor of the faith;[273] seminaries should inculcate in each seminarian a capacity to live in communion with his diocesan bishop.

220 Seminaries should expect of seminarians a spirit of joyful trust, open dialogue, and generous cooperation with those in authority. As seminarians advance in their training, they should be given more opportunity to exercise responsibility and freedom. At the same time, they should understand that accountability is always part of the exercise of freedom.

221 Seminaries should articulate that priestly obedience begins with humble and willing cooperation in seminary life, docility to direction, and wholehearted compliance with the seminary's policies and programs. Seminarians are not expected to surrender their ecclesial rights to express their opinion or to make known their needs.[274] This docility will prepare seminarians to cooperate with their bishop[275] or superior, especially in the very practical matter of undertaking and faithfully fulfilling whatever sacred duty is given to them.[276]

Resources for Human Formation

222 The rector of the seminary has the responsibility to delineate attitudinal and behavioral expectations regarding all aspects of

271 See CIC, c. 750 §2; CCEO, c. 598 §2; St. John Paul II, *Ad Tuendam Fidem*.
272 See CIC, c. 752; CCEO, c. 599.
273 See CIC, c. 753; CCEO, c. 600.
274 CIC, c. 212 §§2-3.
275 See *Presbyterorum Ordinis*, no. 7: "Priests for their part should . . . [respect in their bishop] the authority of Christ the supreme Pastor. They should therefore be attached to their bishop with sincere charity and obedience."
276 See *Christus Dominus*, no. 28.

human formation, especially those appropriate to a life of celibacy, a life of simplicity, and a life of obedience.

223 The community of formators should provide the guidance and direction necessary to help seminarians meet the challenge of emotional and psychosexual growth. In the area of emotional and personal development, the best guidance the seminary formator can give is the wholesome witness of his own life. Seminarians need the example of outstanding priests who model a wholesome way of life in the challenging circumstances of contemporary society. Regularly coming together for prayer, recreation, and theological reflection encourages growth in priestly fraternity and enables priests to act more effectively as authentic role models. The entire seminary staff—composed of priests, consecrated men and women, and lay men and women—constitutes another significant group who can model collaboration for the seminarians. Ways to foster the unity of this larger circle should also be developed.

224 The rector together with the coordinator of human formation should make provision for psychological and counseling services. He therefore ensures that those employed as counselors for seminarians are professionally licensed or certified; are well versed in and supportive of the Church's expectations of seminarians, especially concerning celibacy; and will not encourage behaviors contrary to Church teachings. These services are made available to seminarians for their personal and emotional development as they prepare for the priesthood. The counseling that is given should be consistent with the policy and practice of the total seminary program.

Counseling is often a helpful tool in human formation. Its role, however, should not be overestimated. While psychology and the human sciences are resources that can aid the process of human formation, they are not the same as human formation. Seminaries must draw up guidelines for psychologists, describing objectively those traits and attitudes that indicate satisfactory progress toward the priesthood and those that indicate a lack of the requisite qualities needed for growth in human formation. The basis for such guidelines are the qualities articulated in this *Program of Priestly Formation*. Seminarians in need of long-term therapy should avail themselves of such assistance before entering the seminary or should leave the seminary program until therapy has been completed. If such a departure occurs, there is to be no expectation of automatic readmission. A seminarian should not be considered for advancement to Holy Orders if he is engaged in long-term psychological therapy. Issues being addressed in counseling should be satisfactorily settled prior to the call to Holy Orders. Clear and prudent guidelines are necessary for fostering the personal, emotional, and psychosexual development of seminarians in the context of a wholesome community.

Spiritual Dimension

225 For every Christian, human formation leads to and finds its completion in spiritual formation. Human formation continues in conjunction with and in coordination with the spiritual, intellectual, and pastoral dimensions of formation. "Spiritual formation is directed at nourishing and sustaining communion with God and with our brothers and sisters, in the friendship of Jesus the Good Shepherd, and with an attitude of docility to the Holy Spirit. This intimate relationship forms the heart of the seminarian in that generous and sacrificial love that marks the beginning of pastoral charity."[277]

226 The basic principle of spiritual formation is expressed in *Pastores Dabo Vobis* and is a synthesis of the teachings in *Optatam Totius*: The seminarian is called "to live in intimate and unceasing union with God the Father through his Son Jesus Christ, in the Holy Spirit."[278] This is the foundational call to discipleship and conversion of heart. Those who aspire to be sent on mission, as the Apostles were, must first acquire the listening and learning heart of disciples. Jesus invited these Apostles to come to him before he sent them out to others. St. Augustine alluded to this double identity and commitment as disciple and apostle when he said to his people, "With you I am a Christian, for you I am a bishop."[279]

227 To live in intimate and unceasing union with God the Father through his Son Jesus Christ in the Holy Spirit is far more than a personal or individual relationship with the Lord; it is also a communion with the Church, which is his Body. The spirituality that belongs to those who are priests or preparing for priesthood is at one and the same

277 *Ratio Fundamentalis*, no. 101.
278 *Pastores Dabo Vobis*, no. 45.
279 St. Augustine, *Sermo* 46, 1-2.

time Trinitarian, Christological, pneumatological, and ecclesial. It is a spirituality of communion rooted in the mystery of the Triune God and lived out in practical ways in the mystery of ecclesial communion.

228 The spirituality cultivated in the seminary is specifically priestly. Through the Sacraments of Initiation, seminarians already share in the Paschal Mystery of Jesus Christ with other members of the Church. They also aspire to become priests who are configured to Christ, Head and Shepherd of the Church, our great High Priest. The seminarian is invited to put everything he is and everything he has at the service of the Gospel, deepening his total self-gift through simplicity of life, celibacy and obedience. His interior life gradually draws him deeper into the priestly, self-sacrificial path of Jesus. Jesus is the one whose service finds its high point in giving his life as a ransom for the many,[280] as the Good Shepherd who lays down his life for his sheep "so that they might have life and have it more abundantly,"[281] and as the Bridegroom who loves his Bride, the Church, "and handed himself over for her."[282] Spiritual formation is about forming the heart so that it will interiorize the sentiments and ways of acting of Jesus Christ, the Son of the Father, who always acted in communion with the Holy Spirit.

229 Given these basic dimensions of priestly spirituality that are foundational to the program of spiritual formation in the seminary, the seminary should identify those characteristics and practices that foster its growth. It is a formation that includes the following:

a. *Eucharist*: Spiritual formation is first and foremost a participation in public worship of the Church that is itself a participation in the heavenly Liturgy offered by Christ, our great High Priest. "In the earthly liturgy we take part in a foretaste of that

280 See Mk 10:45.
281 Jn 10:10; see Jn 10:17-18.
282 Eph 5:25; see Eph 5:26-27.

heavenly liturgy which is celebrated in the Holy City of Jerusalem toward which we journey as pilgrims, where Christ is sitting at the right hand of God, Minister of the holies and of the true tabernacle."[283] In the Eucharistic sacrifice, the seminarian learns to offer himself with Christ to the Father and receives spiritual sustenance, Christ's own Flesh and Blood. In Holy Communion, he encounters Jesus Christ, crucified and risen, and opens himself to the transforming power of his self-giving and redeeming love. The Eucharist is the source of pastoral charity, the love that animates and directs those who walk in the footsteps of the Good Shepherd, who gives his life for his sheep so that they may live. As source and summit of the Christian life, the daily celebration of the Eucharist is the essential moment of the day.[284] "The priestly soul strives to make its own what is enacted on the altar of sacrifice. But this cannot be achieved except through priests themselves penetrating ever more intimately through prayer into the mystery of Christ."[285]

b. *Sacrament of Penance*: The Sacrament of Penance fosters the mature recognition of sin, continuous conversion of heart, growth in the virtues, and conformity to the mind of Christ. It is a school of compassion that teaches penitents how to live out God's compassionate mercy in the world. The frequent celebration of the Sacrament of Penance is aided by the practice of a daily examination of conscience.[286]

c. *Liturgy of the Hours*: Through the Liturgy of the Hours (or the Divine Praises, in the Eastern Catholic Churches), seminarians learn to pray with the Church and for the Church, assimilating the language of prayer of the Church that is pleasing to God and transformative, forming both mind and spirit. They unite themselves with the Body of Christ in unceasing praise and petition. This prayer prepares them for their lifelong ministry as priests who pray on behalf of the whole

283 *Sacrosanctum Concilium*, no. 8; see Heb 8:2.
284 See CIC, c. 246 §1; CCEO, c. 346 §2, 2°. See *Pastores Dabo Vobis*, no. 46; *Ecclesia de Eucharistia*.
285 *Presbyterorum Ordinis*, no. 14.
286 See CIC, cc. 246 §4, 276 §2, 5°; CCEO, cc. 369 §1, 346 §2, 4°.

Church. It also cultivates a mind and heart attuned to the whole Body of Christ, its needs, its sufferings, its graces, and its hopes.[287]

d. *Spiritual direction*: Biweekly meetings with an approved spiritual director is an essential part of spiritual direction, especially in arriving at the interiorization and integration needed for growth in sanctity, virtue, and readiness for Holy Orders. Seminaries should offer clear expectations regarding the frequency at which spiritual direction is scheduled.

e. *Bible*: "A relationship with the Word of God holds a preeminent place in the process of spiritual growth."[288] Receiving the Word of God proclaimed and preached in the Church and in the quiet and personal assimilation of that holy word in *lectio divina* enables those in formation to hear God's communication to them as a transforming challenge and hope. To take on more fully the mind of Christ and to be steadily transformed by the Word of God, the seminarian should develop the habit of daily reflection on Sacred Scripture by daily meditation on the lectionary readings and/or other reflective reading of Sacred Scripture.[289]

f. *Retreats and days of recollection*: Regular periods of more intensive prayer will be part of the seminary year.[290] "The annual retreat, a time of profound reflection in prolonged prayerful encounter with the Lord in an atmosphere of silence and recollection, must then be continued during the rest of the year in occasional periods of recollection and in daily prayer."[291]

g. *Personal meditation*: "The heart of spiritual formation is personal union with Christ, which is born of, and nourished in, a particular way by prolonged and silent prayer."[292] The habit of daily prayer and meditation enables seminarians to acquire a personalized sense of how God's salvation has taken hold of their lives and how

287 See CIC, c. 246 §2; CCEO, c. 346 §2, 3°. See *Pastores Dabo Vobis*, no. 48.
288 *Ratio Fundamentalis*, no. 103.
289 See CCEO, c. 346 §2, 1°. See *Pastores Dabo Vobis*, no. 47.
290 See CIC, 246 §5; CCEO, c. 346 §2, 6°.
291 *Ratio Fundamentalis*, no. 108.
292 *Ratio Fundamentalis*, no. 102.

they might respond to that great grace. This prayer happens in a context of silence and solitude in which they learn to be attuned to God's movements in their lives. It grows and develops into a "contemplative attitude" that learns to find God in all things. It matures in such a way that it allows for a balanced and unified rhythm of life in action and contemplation, work and prayer, while providing the future priest with the strength, meaning, and focus he will need in his life.

h. *Praying with the Fathers of the Church*: Studying and meditating on the writings of the Fathers of both the East and the West provide "reliable sources of inspiration" to help address "the emergence of new currents of spirituality" that may be detrimental to the Christian faith or one's vocation.[293]

i. *Devotions*: Devotional prayer, especially centered on Eucharistic Adoration, the Blessed Virgin Mary—in particular the Rosary—and the saints, assists seminarians in assimilating the mystery of Christ and hearing the invitation to live that mystery in the particular circumstances of their own life. Devotional prayer helps to sustain and place in its proper context affective communication with the Lord and his Church. It also helps them to connect with the rich cultural diversity of devotional life in the United States and to appreciate devotional practices of other cultures.[294]

j. *Apostolic dimensions*: "Spiritual formation also involves seeking Christ in people."[295] Especially in a seminary context, seminarians are to learn how prayer is to be lived out in service of others, particularly the poor, the sick, sinners, unbelievers, and the stranger, but extended to all in the outreach of charity and mercy and in the quest for justice. Prayer is apostolic also in the sense that seminarians learn to pray for the needs of those they serve in order to teach others how to pray. Whatever growth and formation in prayer takes place, it is not

293 Congregation for Catholic Education, *Instruction on the Study of the Fathers of the Church in the Formation of Priests*, November 10, 1989, in *Origins* 19:34 (January 25, 1990): 551.
294 See CIC, 246 §3; CCEO, c. 346 §2, 5°. See *Evangelii Gaudium*, nos. 122-126.
295 *Pastores Dabo Vobis*, no. 49.

simply meant for the personal enhancement of the seminarian but as a gift to be given in the course of his priestly mission and ministry for the benefit of the Church—for he is a servant of this body.

k. *Asceticism and penance*: Spiritual formation initiates seminarians to a path of voluntary renunciation and self-denial that makes them more available to the will of God and more available to their people. Asceticism and the practice of penance is a path of learning to embrace the Cross and, in an apostolic context, a way of rendering priests unafraid to bear their "share of hardship for the gospel with the strength that comes from God" (2 Tm 1:8).

l. *Obedience*: The obedience of those in spiritual formation for priesthood must be characterized by the willingness to hear God, who speaks through his Word and through his Church, and to answer his call with generosity. It is also a surrender of one's own will for the sake of the larger mission. In this regard, the seminarian must develop a growing and deepening solidarity with the Church established by Christ; a solidarity with Church teaching so as to be able to present that teaching with conviction—having appropriated it as true; and a solidarity with one's diocesan bishop or superior to strengthen and sustain Church unity.[296]

m. *Celibacy*: Spiritual formation in celibacy cultivates the evangelical motivations for embracing this commitment and way of life: the undivided love of the Lord, the spousal love for the Church, apostolic availability, and the witness to God's promises and Kingdom.[297] A man in formation for ministry must demonstrate the necessary freedom and affective maturity.[298]

---

296 See CIC, cc. 260, 273, 601; CCEO, c. 346 §2, 7°, and 370.

297 See CIC, c. 247 §1. "It is especially important that the priest understand the theological motivation of the Church's law on celibacy. Inasmuch as it is a law, it expresses the Church's will, even before the will of the subject expressed by his readiness. But the will of the Church finds its ultimate motivation in the link between celibacy and sacred ordination, which configures the priest to Jesus Christ the head and spouse of the Church. The Church, as the spouse of Jesus Christ, wishes to be loved by the priest in the total and exclusive manner in which Jesus Christ her head and spouse loved her. Priestly celibacy, then, is the gift of self in and with Christ to his Church and expresses the priest's service to the Church in and with the Lord." *Pastores Dabo Vobis*, no. 29. See also *Pastores Dabo Vobis*, no. 50.

298 See *Ratio Fundamentalis*, no. 110.

n. *Simplicity of life*: Spiritual formation encourages a simple approach to the material goods of this world, cultivating a "spirit of poverty in practical ways."[299] Freed from excessive concern about possessions, priests and seminarians, particularly those in religious institutes and societies of apostolic life, are able to serve in an unencumbered way. To live with evangelical simplicity is to exercise responsible stewardship over God's creation by using material goods in a way that is both responsive to the call of the Gospel and ecologically responsible.[300] The witness of a genuine simplicity of life and of detachment from riches[301] is especially important in the context of affluence in the United States. Spiritual directors and priest formators must be sensitive to seminarians' stewardship of their own, the seminary's, and the Church's material resources. Spiritual formation for simplicity of life and stewardship flows directly from striving to have the mind of Christ Jesus, "who, though he was in the form of God, / did not regard equality with God something to be grasped. / Rather, he emptied himself" (Phil 2:6-7). This is the Lord Jesus who, again according to St. Paul, "for your sake . . . became poor although he was rich, so that by his poverty you might become rich" (2 Cor 8:9).

o. *Reconciliation*: Spiritual formation fosters a reconciling spirit in those who aspire to be priests in the spirit of Jesus, who prayed that "all might be one." A peacemaking and nonviolent way of life marks out those who have been entrusted with the ministry of reconciliation (see 2 Cor 5:18). The power that is entrusted to God's ministers, a power that takes many forms, must always be used for the good, peaceably and in a way that expresses the trust invested in God's priests.

---

299 *Ratio Fundamentalis*, no. 111.

300 See *Laudato Si'*, nos. 216-221. "Living our vocation to be protectors of God's handiwork is essential to a life of virtue; it is not an optional or a secondary aspect of our Christian experience." *Laudato Si'*, no. 217.

301 See *Catechism of the Catholic Church*, no. 2544.

p. *Solidarity*: The post-synodal apostolic exhortation *Ecclesia in America* identified the critical importance of the path of solidarity for the Church in the Americas.

> "Solidarity is thus the fruit of the communion which is grounded in the mystery of the Triune God, and in the Son of God who took flesh and died for all. It is expressed in Christian love which seeks the good of others, especially of those most in need." For the particular Churches of the American continent, this is the source of a commitment to reciprocal solidarity and the sharing of the spiritual gifts and material goods with which God has blessed them, fostering in individuals a readiness to work where they are needed.[302]

This means that seminarians are to have a spiritual formation grounded in Trinitarian communion that leads them to solidarity with others, especially those most in need; to a commitment to justice and peace; to a reciprocal exchange of spiritual and material gifts; and to an authentic missionary spirit, expressed in a willingness to serve where needed.

q. *Solitude*: Spiritual formation must not neglect the art of "being alone with God," moving the man from being alone or lonely to entering a holy solitude in communion with God.

r. *A life of discernment*: The *Ratio Fundamentalis* describes well how all of these means of spiritual growth help the seminarian to establish a life of discernment: "The gradual inner growth along the journey of formation should principally be aimed at making the future priest a 'man of discernment,' able to read the reality of human life in the light of the Spirit." This discernment applies first to one's personal life: "It is necessary to integrate one's own personal situation and history into the spiritual life. . . . Discerning one's life according to the Gospel means cultivating every day a deep spiritual life, so as to receive it and interpret it with full responsibility and a growing trust in God, directing the heart towards him each day." It extends

302 *Ecclesia in America*, no. 52.

ultimately to the pastoral life so "he will be able to choose, decide and act according to the will of God." All of the means included here "help to cultivate the virtues of prudence and right judgment. In this ongoing path of discernment the priest will learn how to interpret and understand his own motivations, his gifts, his needs and his frailties, so as to 'free himself from all disordered affections and, having removed them, to seek out and find the will of God in the ordering of his life with a view to the salvation of the soul.'"[303]

s. *Ongoing spiritual formation*: The final goal of spiritual formation in the seminary is to establish attitudes, habits, and practices in the spiritual life that will continue after ordination. Spiritual formation in the seminary is meant to set the foundation for a lifetime of spiritual growth in priestly ministry.

230 The development of sound and lasting habits and attitudes in the spiritual life is a challenging process. Intensive spiritual formation experiences—such as an extended time period more exclusively focused on the interior life, a thirty-day retreat, a summer program, and so on—are examples of facilitating this process and may be considered for possible inclusion and integration into the seminary program.

231 Spiritual formation needs to be integrated with the other three dimensions of formation—the human, the intellectual, and the pastoral. The necessary growth in the theological and moral virtues involves both nature and grace. The necessary integration takes place when spiritual directors and priest formators work from a common vision of the relationship between grace and virtue. Spiritual formation also requires that the seminarian have a strong relational capacity. In other words, the seminarian must be able to enter into

303 *Ratio Fundamentalis*, no. 43. Here the *Ratio Fundamentalis* notes the particular value of the Ignatian rules of discernment.

significant, even deep, relationships with other persons and with God, since he is to be a "man of communion."[304]

232 Intellectual formation contributes to spiritual formation by helping the seminarian grow in the love of the truth, who is the person of Jesus Christ. This love gives the seminarian the capacity to discern and understand his interior life within the life of the Church and her Tradition. Growth in knowledge of God and of his saving works can strengthen the seminarian's faith, hope, and charity. Likewise, the study of the traditions and the experiences of faith among the saints and the People of God serves to deepen one's own spiritual journey.

233 Pastoral formation is intimately linked with spiritual formation. In the process of spiritual formation, men are formed to receive the love of God in such a way that they desire to share that love by making a gift of their entire lives. As their hearts are gradually formed in the image of Christ, the Good Shepherd and Bridegroom, their interior life becomes a source of pastoral charity that enables them to lay down their lives generously in service of others. "This intimate relationship forms the heart of the seminarian in that generous and sacrificial love that marks the beginning of pastoral charity."[305] In this the seminarian learns to eschew any false independence in his labors and to live the words of Jesus: "without me you can do nothing" (Jn 15:5).

234 It is important that spiritual formation is integrated with the other three dimensions of formation such that all formation allows the future priest to embrace pastoral charity as central to his ministry.[306] Human, intellectual, and pastoral formation are equally indispensable in developing the seminarian's relationship and communion with God and his ability to communicate to others, in pastoral charity,

304 "The Eucharist commits us to the poor. To receive in truth the Body and Blood of Christ given up for us, we must recognize Christ in the poorest." *Catechism of the Catholic Church*, no. 1397.
305 *Ratio Fundamentalis*, no. 101.
306 See *Presbyterorum Ordinis*, no. 14.

God's truth and love in the likeness of Jesus Christ, the Good Shepherd and eternal High Priest.

PROPAEDEUTIC STAGE BENCHMARKS

235 One of the primary objectives of the propaedeutic stage is to provide an introduction to the spiritual life and to develop a solid foundation in the seminarian's life of prayer. Those elements in the spiritual dimension to be achieved prior to beginning the discipleship stage include growth in prayer and the spiritual life (e.g., elementary discipline in public and private prayer, interest in and attention to spiritual direction, understanding of the importance of silence, and a growing habit of silence), growth in an understanding of the celibate life (e.g., ability to articulate the Church's understanding of the promise of celibacy and the spiritual motivation for celibacy, growth in the virtue of chastity, and growth in the habit of healthy solitude), growth in the understanding of the priestly vocation, the ability to articulate a relationship with Jesus Christ, and growth in reading and meditating on Sacred Scripture.

DISCIPLESHIP STAGE BENCHMARKS

236 In the discipleship stage, the seminarian demonstrates a growing openness to the Holy Spirit as the primary agent of formation in his life; he recognizes God's grace enabling him to grow and discern with the grateful assistance of his formators. The seminarian continues to learn from Christ the Good Shepherd to do as he does. His deepening friendship with Jesus Christ and his understanding of the Good Shepherd's call to ordained ministry will allow him to enter the next stage confident in his vocation to the priesthood. He develops greater insight into why he feels God is calling him to the priesthood and why he desires priesthood.

237 Spiritual benchmarks related to prayer and the spiritual life that the seminarian should achieve by the end of the discipleship stage include consistent participation in communal spiritual exercises and liturgies, including prayerful participation in the Mass and Divine Office (or the Divine Praises, in the Eastern Catholic Churches); a demonstrated habit of regular spiritual reading; the ability to speak with facility about God's work in his life; and a habit of personal prayer, spiritual direction, and participation in the Sacrament of Penance.

238 By the end of the discipleship stage, the seminarian is able to articulate his understanding and awareness of God's call to him of a lifelong commitment to celibate chastity.[307] He continues to grow in the virtue of chastity. He has the ability to articulate and demonstrate appropriate boundaries with others, relating to all persons as beloved children of the Father, and possesses a solid understanding and desire of a habit of healthy solitude. He demonstrates a growing transparency in his relationship with Jesus Christ through his ability to describe this relationship to others in a meaningful way; he nurtures this relationship through a well-established habit of reading and meditating on Sacred Scripture.

CONFIGURATION STAGE BENCHMARKS

239 The well-established friendship between the seminarian and Jesus Christ, which is necessarily characteristic of the man by the end of the configuration stage, is reflected in an internalized habit of reading and meditating on Sacred Scripture, as well as the ability to identify and communicate connections between meditation on

307 This includes a growing understanding of the positive reasons for a lifelong commitment to celibate chastity. St. Paul VI articulates these as "a real participation in His [Christ's] own unique priesthood. . . . Christ remained throughout His whole life in the state of celibacy, which signified His total dedication to the service of God and men." *Sacerdotalis Caelibatus* (*On the Celibacy of the Priest*, 1967), nos. 19, 21; see also no. 23, *www.vatican.va/content/paul-vi/en/encyclicals/documents/hf_p-vi_enc_24061967_sacerdotalis.html*. In addition to raising matrimony to the dignity of a sacrament, Christ "has also opened a new way, in which the human creature adheres wholly and directly to the Lord, and is concerned only with Him and with His affairs" (*Sacerdotalis Caelibatus*, no. 20). The "free choice of sacred celibacy . . . stimulates to a charity which is open to all" and "manifests the virginal love of Christ for the Church" (*Sacerdotalis Caelibatus*, nos. 24, 26).

Sacred Scripture, his relationship with Christ, and his personal spiritual growth. This friendship can be seen in his ability to live a simple life and articulate the reasons for it. He is able to recognize and articulate concretely God's grace active in his life and the lives of others, identifying in common life that *communio* which enriches and deepens his life with Christ for the sake of others.

240 He demonstrates an ability to maintain fidelity to the Liturgy of the Hours (or the Divine Praises, in the Eastern Catholic Churches), daily Mass, and personal prayer, both in the seminary or religious house and away from those structures. Thus he demonstrates that his spiritual life has been internalized and that he is not only fulfilling external requirements. He can assist others in their spiritual growth through a prayerful familiarity with God's Word and the spiritual Tradition of the Church.

241 By the end of the configuration stage, the seminarian can live the virtue of chastity and can communicate a free and joyful lifelong commitment to celibate chastity. With the ever-deepening awareness of his own humanity, with its gifts and limitations, he can recognize common and personal causes of loneliness and can develop a habit of healthy approaches to these challenges and improve his habit of solitude.[308]

242 From the standpoint of his vocation, the seminarian can communicate a presumption of permanence to priesthood and share his joyful desire for lifelong priestly life and ministry, as well as a desire to live the sacramental life of a priest. He understands the importance of the

---

308 Healthy habits in this area are crucial to his future well-being as a priest. "The *Causes and Context* data indicate that abuse is most likely to occur at times of stress, loneliness, and isolation. Such stressful or challenging situations triggered the desire in some priests to form inappropriate relationships with others—such relationships were most often with adults, but sometimes with minors." John Jay College Research Team, *The Causes and Context of Sexual Abuse of Minors by Catholic Priests in the United States, 1950-2010: A Report Presented to the United States Conference of Catholic Bishops* (Washington, DC: USCCB, 2011), 120.

evangelical counsels for priestly life. He manifests the identity of the priesthood—Head and Shepherd, Servant and Spouse.

VOCATIONAL SYNTHESIS STAGE BENCHMARKS

243 In this stage, the transitional deacon continues to grow in the solid foundations of prayer, discernment, and solitude as he moves to full-time ministry in the parish. It is important that during the vocational synthesis stage he continues to maintain his regular habits of spiritual direction, daily Mass, and personal prayer, demonstrating the ability to integrate into his own internal spiritual and prayer life his pastoral experiences and the people to whom he ministers. A formal process of theological reflection will aid this effort.

244 His continued growth in the pursuit of holiness, essential to his priesthood, is aided through his faithful pursuit of ministry.[309] Demonstrating an obedient heart in his pastoral assignment and in his relationship with his bishop and pastor, or with the competent authority of an institute of consecrated life or society of apostolic life, is necessary for his future happiness as a priest. So too, his recognizing the need for appropriate and regular communication with his bishop, vicar general, and other diocesan officials or competent superiors is a way of demonstrating that he understands the spirit of an obedient priestly heart.

245 To continue his growth in the virtue of chastity and strengthen his celibate commitment, it is vital that the transitional deacon demonstrate the ability to recognize and discuss potentially unhealthy relationships in ministry, not simply in generic terms but personally. This will assist him in having the necessary ability to maintain appropriate boundaries and safeguards in pastoral settings. Demonstrating the ability to spend time alone in his pastoral setting and continuing to master a

309 See CIC, c. 276 §2, 1°; *Presbyterorum Ordinis*, nos. 12-14.

healthy habit of fruitful solitude with himself and God are necessary benchmarks to achieve prior to ordination to the priesthood.

Norms for Spiritual Formation

Prayer

246 The celebration of the Eucharist takes place daily, and every member of the community ordinarily participates.[310] This includes a regularly scheduled Saturday morning Mass and Sunday community Mass. All priests who are not bound to celebrate individually for the pastoral benefit of the faithful should concelebrate at the community Mass insofar as possible.[311] In like manner, unless excused for a just reason, it is preferable that priests concelebrate when they are present for Mass.

247 The seminary community must schedule the Liturgy of the Hours (or the Divine Praises, in the Eastern Catholic Churches), especially Morning and Evening Prayers, on a daily basis.[312]

248 The careful preparation and execution of liturgical celebrations should be supervised by the seminary coordinator of the liturgy. Because the liturgical life of the seminary shapes the sensitivities and attitudes of seminarians for future ministry, an authentic sense of the holy mysteries should be carefully preserved in all liturgical celebrations, along with a care for their beauty and dignity.[313] The laws and prescriptions of approved liturgical books are normative. Priests are to be particularly observant of the liturgical rubrics and must avoid the insertion of any personal liturgical adaptations, unless they are authorized by the liturgical books.[314] The seminary liturgy should also promote in seminarians a respect for legitimate,

310 See CIC, c. 246 §1; CCEO, c. 346 §2, 2°; *Ratio Fundamentalis*, no. 104. In regard to the frequency of the celebration of the Eucharist, those seminaries forming men for Eastern Catholic Churches are to develop a schedule of liturgical services that best represents common liturgical practice in the jurisdictions they serve.

311 See *General Instruction of the Roman Missal*, no. 114.

312 See CIC, c. 246 §2; CCEO, c. 346 §2, 3°; *Ratio Fundamentalis*, no. 105.

313 See *Ecclesia de Eucharistia*, no. 5.

314 See *Ecclesia de Eucharistia*, no. 52.

rubrically approved liturgical expressions of cultural diversity as well as the Church's ancient liturgical patrimony.[315] Seminaries in the Latin Church should include in their liturgies Gregorian chant, as the chant proper to the Roman Liturgy, as well as the forms of chant in the particular Churches.[316] Priests should always be aware that they have a particular and serious responsibility to model for seminarians the proper way to preside at the sacraments, especially the Eucharist, including concelebration. All other teachers of the liturgy as well as coordinators of music at the seminary are to be supportive of this norm.

249 Meditation on Sacred Scripture holds pride of place in the personal prayer regimen of each seminarian, traditionally experienced as *lectio divina*. Deepening one's friendship with Jesus Christ necessarily involves daily meditation on the Word of God, in addition to the public prayer and liturgy in the seminary and other forms of private prayer and devotions.[317]

250 Instruction is to be given concerning the meaning and proper celebration of the Eucharist and the Liturgy of the Hours (or the Divine Praises, in the Eastern Catholic Churches) as well as their benefits for spiritual growth in the seminary and for the communities that seminarians later will serve. Seminarians must be instructed to incorporate progressively all of the hours of the Liturgy of the Hours or the Divine Praises, beginning with Morning Prayer and Evening Prayer, the Office of Readings, and finally the Daytime Hour and Night Prayer. This entire cycle should be a regular practice of each seminarian for at least a year prior to his diaconate ordination.

251 Catechesis must be given concerning the Sacrament of Penance and its importance for priestly ministry and life. Communal celebrations of

315 See *Ecclesia de Eucharistia*, nos. 49-51; *General Instruction of the Roman Missal*, no. 41.
316 See *Sacramentum Caritatis*, no. 62.
317 See *Ratio Fundamentalis*, no. 103.

the Sacrament of Penance with individual confession and absolution should be scheduled regularly, especially during Advent and Lent. The seminary must schedule frequent opportunities at various times during the week and encourage the individual celebration of the Sacrament of Penance. In addition to regular confessors, the seminary should ensure that other confessors for the Sacrament of Penance are available on a regular basis.[318] A priest who has sole responsibility for external formation is not to hear seminarians' confessions. Opinions of the spiritual director or confessor of a seminarian may never be sought regarding his advancement.[319] Each seminarian is encouraged to have a regular confessor, who fittingly is also his spiritual director, with whom he can be completely honest and fully manifest his conscience, and from whom he can receive ongoing guidance.[320] This is not meant to limit the seminarian's liberty, since he is always free to approach other confessors, whether in the seminary or outside it.[321]

252 The seminary program and spiritual direction should teach seminarians to value solitude and personal prayer as a necessary part of priestly spirituality. Occasions for silence and properly directed solitude should be provided during retreats and days of recollection. An atmosphere of quiet should be provided within the seminary community on a daily basis to ensure an environment conducive for prayer.

253 Conferences, days of recollection, workshops, and retreats should be well organized and sponsored by the seminary and should form a whole and coherent program of spiritual formation. An annual retreat lasting at least five days must take place during the configuration stage.[322]

---

318 See CIC, c. 240 §1; CCEO, c. 339 §2.
319 See CIC, c. 240 §2; CCEO, c. 339 §3.
320 See CIC, c. 246 §4.
321 See CIC, c. 240 §1; CCEO, c. 339 §2.
322 See CIC, c. 1039; CCEO, c. 772.

254 Guidance and instruction in methods of meditation, contemplation, *lectio divina*, daily examen, and meditation on the Fathers of the Church must be provided.[323]

255 Devotion to the Blessed Sacrament must be encouraged. Scheduled hours of Eucharistic Exposition are particularly desirable to provide special opportunities for the Adoration of the Blessed Sacrament in the seminary. It is also desirable that seminarians develop a habit of personal visits to the Blessed Sacrament in the tabernacle.[324]

256 Devotion to the Blessed Virgin Mary, the Mother of God, and to the saints must be encouraged.[325] Opportunities for devotional prayer should be made available and encouraged. The Rosary, "a compendium of the Gospel,"[326] is especially recommended as a means of contemplating Christ in "the school of Mary."[327] Devotion to the other saints, especially St. Joseph, is also an important element of the devotional life of seminarians and priests.[328]

257 On appropriate occasions, the seminary should sponsor ecumenical events, including prayer services, with other Christians. Consideration should also be given to interaction with those of the Jewish faith and other religions.

258 The seminary should provide seminarians with training on the proper use of sacramentals, including consecrations, blessings, and reverence for sacred things.[329]

---

323 See CIC, c. 246 §3; CCEO, c. 346 §2, 1°; see *Ratio Fundamentalis*, no. 113.
324 See Sacred Congregation for Divine Worship, *Holy Communion and Worship of the Eucharist Outside of Mass*, nos. 79-81.
325 See CIC, c. 246 §3; CCEO, c. 346 §2, 5°.
326 Pope Pius XII, letter *Philippinas insulas* to the Archbishop of Manila, AAS 38 (1946): 419. See St. Paul VI, *Marialis Cultus* (1974), no. 42, *www.vatican.va/content/paul-vi/en/apost_exhortations/documents/hf_p-vi_exh_19740202_marialis-cultus.html*; *Rosarium Virginis Mariae*, no. 1.
327 *Rosarium Virginis Mariae*, no. 1.
328 See *Ratio Fundamentalis*, no. 112.
329 See CIC, cc. 1166-1172.

Spiritual Direction

259 Seminarians must meet regularly with a priest spiritual director, normally biweekly.[330] The seminarian freely chooses an available spiritual director from a list prepared by the coordinator of spiritual formation. Spiritual directors should have proper training and adequate credentials for the work. These priests must be approved by the rector and appointed by the competent authority.[331] Spiritual direction should be offered in the language that allows the seminarian to best express himself. In the case of seminarians of an institute of consecrated life or society of apostolic life, the formation director or the competent authority of the institute or society offers guidance on an appropriate spiritual director for the seminarians under his care.

260 Seminarians should confide their personal history, personal relationships, prayer experiences, cultivation of virtues, temptations, and other significant topics to their spiritual director. If, for serious reason, there is a change of director, the new director should give attention to continuity in the seminarian's spiritual development.

330 See CIC, c. 246 §4; CCEO, c. 346 §2, 4°.
331 See CIC, c. 239 §2; CCEO, c. 339 §1.

Intellectual Dimension

261 There is a reciprocal relationship between spiritual and intellectual formation. The intellectual life nourishes the spiritual life, but the spiritual also opens vistas of understanding, in accordance with the classical adage *credo ut intelligam* (I believe in order to understand). Intellectual formation is integral to what it means to be human.

262 "To ensure the adequate intellectual formation of future priests, all disciplines must be taught in such a way as to make their intimate connection stand out clearly, avoiding fragmentation. It is to be a unified, integral journey, in which each subject is an important 'tile in the mosaic' for presenting the mystery of Christ and the Church, and for allowing an authentic Christian vision of man and the world to mature."[332]

263 The basic principle of intellectual formation for seminarians is noted in *Pastores Dabo Vobis*: "For the salvation of their brothers and sisters they should seek an ever deeper knowledge of the divine mysteries."[333] Disciples are learners. The first task of intellectual formation is to acquire a personal knowledge of the Lord Jesus Christ, who is the fullness and completion of God's Revelation and the one Teacher. This saving knowledge is not acquired only once but rather is continuously appropriated and deepened, so that it becomes more and more part of the disciple. Seminary intellectual formation assumes and prolongs the catechesis and mystagogia that is to be part of every Christian's journey of faith. At the same time, this knowledge is not simply for personal possession but is destined to be shared in the community of faith; that is why it is "for the salvation of their brothers and sisters." Intellectual formation has an apostolic and missionary purpose and finality.

332 *Ratio Fundamentalis*, no. 153.
333 *Pastores Dabo Vobis*, no. 51.

264 In the seminary program, intellectual formation culminates in a deepened understanding of the mysteries of faith that is pastorally oriented toward effective priestly ministry, especially preaching, which is "the touchstone for judging a pastor's closeness and ability to communicate to his people."[334] This understanding, however, requires previous intellectual formation and academic integrity as foundational. The overall goal of every stage of seminary formation is to prepare a seminarian who is widely knowledgeable about the human condition, deeply engaged in a process of understanding Divine Revelation, and adequately skilled in communicating his knowledge to as many people as possible. Moreover, continuing education after ordination is a necessity for effective ministry.

265 Intellectual formation must be directed to the ecclesial dimensions of priestly formation, namely, the teaching office (*munus docendi*) of the priesthood. The doctrinal, educational, catechetical, and apologetical aspects of training are to prepare the seminarian to be a faithful, loyal, and authentic teacher of the Gospel. As a man of the Church, the priest preaches and teaches in fidelity to the Magisterium, particularly the Holy Father and the diocesan bishop. The intellectual formation program must emphasize the intrinsic relationship between the knowledge gained in theological preparation and the ecclesial dimensions of priestly service, since the education of a priest is never seen in isolation from the Tradition of the Church.

266 The context of intellectual formation in the United States during the twenty-first century is important to note, because it highlights the specific challenges that both seminaries and seminarians face in the process of intellectual formation. Among the elements of context are the following:

a. Many men approach the seminary with a significant educational background. They are, however, often narrowly educated; that is,

334 *Evangelii Gaudium*, no. 135.

they may have great expertise in a particular area and have a high level of technical training but lack a wide background. Often lacking is education in the humanities, which would enable them to study theology effectively and make pastoral connections with the lives of the people whom they will serve.

b. Older men approach the seminary with considerable life experience, but they may have lost contact with formal patterns of study in school. Their age may seem to warrant that they be moved through the seminarian program quickly, or that they be given a program that has been reduced in expectations. This latter trend, however, is to be resisted.

c. Men with an international background may arrive at the seminary with a limited knowledge of the English language as well as a limited understanding of US culture. These limitations present significant challenges for teaching and learning. Unless the seminarian has sufficient familiarity with language and culture, his study of theology will be severely impeded.[335]

d. Men coming from a US cultural context, even though they may be young and have had exposure to the liberal arts in college, may bring with them the limitations of the culture's understanding of the human person as well as the limitations of a philosophical milieu that is suspicious of or even rejects enduring, absolute moral values and objective truths. Unless these men are grounded in an adequate philosophical and theological anthropology, they will struggle to make sense of their theological studies and their application in pastoral practice.

e. Men apply to seminary programs with backgrounds of varied religious experiences and varied levels of catechetical formation.

267 "Intellectual formation is a part of the integral formation of the priest. Moreover, it serves his pastoral ministry and has an impact upon his human and spiritual formation, which draw rich nourishment from

335 See *Guidelines for Receiving Pastoral Ministers in the United States* cited earlier in the propaedeutic stage section for more information on reception and orientation of men from international backgrounds.

it."[336] Intellectual formation applies not only to a comprehensive understanding of the mysteries of the Catholic faith, but also to an ability to explain and even defend the reasoning that supports those truths. In this way, intellectual formation provides those who are being formed spiritually with a knowledge of the Lord and his ways, which they embrace in faith. Finally, intellectual formation through the study of theology enables priests to contemplate, share, and communicate the mysteries of faith with others. In this way, it has an essentially pastoral orientation.

THE PROPAEDEUTIC STAGE

268 The propaedeutic stage is "an ideal opportunity to acquire an initial and overall familiarity with Christian doctrine by studying the *Catechism of the Catholic Church*."[337] Teaching new seminarians the basics of priestly identity and spirituality is also a chief aim of the intellectual formation of this stage. Seminarians should obtain an introductory knowledge of the Bible that equips them to thoughtfully read and pray with Sacred Scripture. Training in intercultural competency, including beginning to learn a new language to meet the pastoral needs of the diocese, should be included in the intellectual formation of seminarians.

269 Other areas of study that support this broad foundational doctrinal formation could include introduction to the documents of the Second Vatican Council and other principal documents of the Magisterium, introductory reading of the Church Fathers and Doctors, and study of the lives the saints and blesseds (especially American saints and blesseds).[338] In addition, intellectual formation could begin to familiarize the seminarian with the great schools of spiritual theology and the spiritual masters.

336 *Ratio Fundamentalis*, no. 117.
337 *Ratio Fundamentalis*, no. 59.
338 See *Ratio Fundamentalis*, no. 157.

270 For international seminarians, English-language study (for those for whom English is not the primary language) and an acculturation program should be completed prior to beginning the propaedeutic stage. Continued study of English and acculturation during the propaedeutic stage is also vital. It is helpful, and sometimes necessary, that spiritual direction and some human formation during this stage be provided in the first or primary language of the seminarian to allow for adequate vocational discernment.[339]

PROPAEDEUTIC STAGE BENCHMARKS

271 Gaining an initial understanding of Christian doctrine and anthropology as well as an initial familiarity of the Bible in its various parts are benchmarks that should be reached prior to embarking on philosophical studies in the discipleship stage.[340] Benchmarks related to intellectual formation in preparation for the study of philosophy and theology include basic habits of study, signs of intellectual curiosity, and love of learning. Finally, if necessary, the propaedeutic stage can help to make up for anything that is missing in a seminarian's general education.[341]

THE DISCIPLESHIP STAGE

272 A great number of seminarians enter the discipleship stage with a wealth of education and practical experience, yet many younger men enter discipleship stage with minimal or no higher education. The seminary intellectual program must meet the various needs of these men. All men in the discipleship stage must receive philosophical formation to train their minds in right reason and prepare them to study theology. In addition, as future pastors and leaders, these seminarians need to be broadly educated in order to develop as Christian men and engage with society. Thus, the discipleship stage envisions benchmarks for

339 See *Ratio Fundamentalis*, no. 27.
340 See *Ratio Fundamentalis*, no. 157.
341 See *Ratio Fundamentalis*, no. 59.

intellectual formation with two aspects: a broad grasp of the liberal arts and sciences, and particular knowledge of philosophy. Seminarians who enter the discipleship stage in possession of a broader intellectual formation (for example, with an undergraduate degree or more extensive education) may have already met the benchmarks for the liberal arts and sciences and will not need formation in this aspect but will focus on philosophy. Seminarians beginning the discipleship stage with minimal education beyond secondary school will need to pursue a liberal arts education as well as philosophical studies and should achieve a baccalaureate degree before beginning the configuration stage. The discipleship stage program promotes intellectual excellence and takes necessary steps to help seminarians to achieve it.

273 Men who enter seminary without a substantial liberal arts education follow a twofold course of intellectual formation. They first pursue the liberal arts, through which they acquire a sense of the great human questions and the responses to them presented in the arts and sciences. Then they also synthesize and organize their study of the liberal arts through the study of philosophy, which also serves as a preparation for the study of theology.

Liberal Arts

274 A sound liberal arts education for seminarians provides multiple benefits. The study of the natural world and of humanity in all its historical and cultural diversity represents a significant value in its own right. Such an education encourages intellectual curiosity, promotes critical thought, and fosters disciplined habits of study, but above all it aims to hand on the truths about God and his creation that are the foundation of civilization. A liberal arts education also teaches seminarians to communicate with others in a clear and effective way.

275 A liberal arts education gives seminarians an introduction to the wider range of human learning. Studies in mathematics and natural sciences; in the social and behavioral sciences; in history, literature, foreign languages—both ancient (Latin and Greek) and modern; and in communication skills, music, and the fine arts all define the content of a liberal arts curriculum.

276 A liberal arts education also has a special value as a preparation for the study of theology. The liberal arts have traditionally provided seminarians with an understanding of the cultural roots of their faith. By understanding the human sciences, they can comprehend better the world in which God acts. By grasping how faith and culture have interacted in the past, they gain some insight into the working of God's plan in larger historical events.

277 The curriculum should also strive to take into consideration contemporary issues of the day in intellectual, cultural, social, economic, and political life as they pertain to moral and religious topics. Such an approach stimulates seminarians to deeper study by building on current knowledge and interests. The authentic social doctrine of the Church on such issues should be clearly and cogently presented.[342] The curriculum should introduce seminarians to the basic teachings of the faith as well as to the richness and diversity of the wisdom attained in the Catholic intellectual tradition.

PHILOSOPHY

278 All seminarians in the discipleship stage study philosophy. Men who come to the discipleship stage in possession of a broader intellectual formation must engage in the full philosophical intellectual formation program outlined below. The study of philosophy is central to the intellectual formation of seminarians. The temptation to abbreviate

342 See *Ratio Fundamentalis*, no. 172.

or circumvent requirements for seminarians in these circumstances must be avoided.

279 "The study of philosophy is fundamental and indispensable to the structure of theological studies and to the formation of candidates for the priesthood [or seminarians]. It is not by chance that the curriculum of theological studies is preceded by a time of special study of philosophy."[343] In priestly formation, at least two full years must be dedicated to the philosophical disciplines, which corresponds to the two-year period of the discipleship stage and composes a major aspect of intellectual formation.[344] The particular focus of intellectual formation, as well as the other dimensions of formation during this period, is to help the seminarian deepen his identity as a disciple of Jesus Christ.

280 There is an "intimate bond which ties theological work to the philosophical search for truth."[345] It is essential that seminarians develop an understanding of the relationship between faith and reason and of the relationship and interaction between philosophy and theology, especially the ways they mutually enrich one another. "A proper philosophical training is vital, not only because of the links between the great philosophical questions and the mysteries of salvation which are studied in theology under the guidance of the higher light of faith, but also vis-à-vis an extremely widespread cultural situation which emphasizes subjectivism as a criterion and measure of truth: Only a sound philosophy can help candidates for the priesthood to develop a reflective awareness of the fundamental relationship that exists between the human spirit and truth, that truth which is revealed to us fully in Jesus Christ."[346]

281 The study of philosophy is not just part of intellectual formation but is also connected to human, spiritual, and pastoral formation.

---

343 *Fides et Ratio*, no. 62.
344 See CIC, c. 250; CCEO, c. 348 §1.
345 *Fides et Ratio*, no. 63.
346 *Pastores Dabo Vobis*, no. 52.

Issues about priestly identity and about the apostolic and missionary dimensions of priestly ministry "are closely linked to the question about the nature of truth." Philosophy serves "as a guarantee of that 'certainty of truth' which is the only firm basis for a total giving of oneself to Jesus and to the Church."[347]

282 The seminary philosophy program of studies should be balanced, comprehensive, integrated, and coherent. The philosophy program must include substantial studies in the history of philosophy, treating of ancient, medieval, modern, and contemporary philosophy.

a. The study of the history of philosophy helps seminarians understand philosophical issues as they have developed in the Western philosophical tradition and, more particularly, in the Catholic intellectual tradition, which has been both shaped by and contributed to the shape of the Western philosophical tradition. This historical approach to the study of philosophy aids in the "integration of philosophical studies . . . [through] a specific 'philosophical methodology.'"[348] The knowledge of philosophy, with its powerful impact on theology and theologians, is necessary in order to appreciate the richness of our theological Tradition.

b. At the same time, philosophy prepares seminarians for priestly ministry. By living more reflectively in the historical Catholic intellectual tradition, seminarians are better equipped for their ministry of teaching the faith, better prepared to engage contemporary culture, and better prepared for the "evangelization of culture" that is integral to the new evangelization. In this regard, some treatment of American philosophy or social thought is also helpful for seminarians in understanding the dynamics of contemporary society in the United States.[349]

---

347 *Pastores Dabo Vobis*, no. 52.

348 *Ratio Fundamentalis*, no. 159.

349 For example, see the following resources from the USCCB: *Bishops' Program for Social Reconstruction* (1919); *The Challenge of Peace* (1983); *Economic Justice for All* (1986); *Called to Global Solidarity* (1997); *Responsibility, Rehabilitation, and Restoration: A Catholic Perspective on Crime and Criminal Justice* (2000); *Global Climate Change: A Plea for Dialogue, Prudence and the Common Good* (2001); *Strangers No Longer: Together on a Journey of Hope* (2003); and *Forming Consciences for Faithful Citizenship* (2015). Pontifical Biblical Commission, *The Bible and Morality: Biblical Roots of Christian Conduct* (2008), is also a resource.

283 The philosophy program must include the study of logic, epistemology, philosophy of nature, metaphysics, natural theology, anthropology, and ethics:

a. The study of logic helps seminarians to develop their critical and analytical abilities and become clearer thinkers who will be better able rationally to present, discuss, and defend the truths of the faith.

b. The study of epistemology, the investigation of the nature and properties of knowledge, helps seminarians see "that human knowledge is capable of gathering from contingent reality objective and necessary truths,"[350] while recognizing also the limits of human knowledge. Moreover, it reinforces their understanding of the relationship between reason and Revelation. They come to appreciate the power of reason to know the truth; yet as they confront the limits of the powers of human reason, they are opened to look to Revelation for a fuller knowledge of those truths that exceed the power of human reason.

c. The study of the philosophy of nature—which treats of fundamental principles like substance, form, matter, causality, motion, and the soul—provides seminarians a foundation for the study of metaphysics, natural theology, anthropology, and ethics.

d. The study of metaphysics helps seminarians to explore fundamental issues concerning the nature of reality and to see that reality and truth transcend the empirical. "A philosophy which shuns metaphysics would be radically unsuited to the task of mediation in the understanding of Revelation."[351] As the seminarian confronts the questions about being itself, he gains a deeper understanding and appreciation of God as the source of all being and gains some sense of how profound is this truth. A strong background in metaphysics also gives him the structure and ability to discuss certain theological concepts that depend on metaphysics for their articulation and explanation.

350 Congregation for Catholic Education, *The Study of Philosophy in Seminaries* (1972).
351 *Fides et Ratio*, no. 83.

e. The study of natural theology, which treats of the existence of God and the attributes of God by means of the natural light of reason, provides a foundation for the seminarian's study of theology and the knowledge of God by means of Revelation.

f. The study of philosophical anthropology helps seminarians understand "the authentic spirituality of man, leading to a theocentric ethic, transcending earthly life, and at the same time open to the social dimension of man."[352] The philosophical study of the human "person, his fulfillment in intersubjectivity, his destiny, his inalienable rights, [and] his 'nuptial character' as one of the primary elements which is expressive of human nature and constitutive of society"[353] provides a foundation for the seminarian's study of theological anthropology.

g. The study of ethics, which treats of general principles of ethical decision making, provides seminarians with a solid grounding in themes like conscience, freedom, law, responsibility, virtue, and guilt. Ethics also considers the common good and virtue of solidarity as central to Christian social political philosophy. Ethics should consider the Church's social doctrine as central to Christian social political philosophy.[354] The social encyclicals and other documents foundational to the Church's rich social doctrine should be utilized in the study of ethics. These principles and documents provide a foundation for the seminarian's study of moral theology.[355]

284 "Philosophical instruction must be grounded in the perennially valid philosophical heritage and also take into account philosophical investigation over the course of time. It is to be taught in such a

352 See Congregation for Catholic Education, *The Study of Philosophy in Seminaries* (1972).

353 Congregation for Catholic Education, *Directives Regarding the Formation of Seminarians for Ministry to Marriage and Family* (1995), no. 21, *www.usccb.org/beliefs-and-teachings/vocations/priesthood/priestly-formation/upload/marriage.pdf*.

354 See *Compendium of the Social Doctrine of the Church*, nos. 160-208.

355 See Pope Leo XIII, *Rerum Novarum* (1891); Pope Pius XI, *Quadragesimo Anno* (1931); St. John XXIII, *Mater et Magistra* (1961); St. John XXIII, *Pacem in Terris* (1963); Second Vatican Council, *Gaudium et Spes* (1965); St. Paul VI, *Populorum Progressio* (1967); St. Paul VI, *Octogesima Adveniens* (1971); St. John Paul II, *Laborem Exercens* (1981); St. John Paul II, *Sollicitudo Rei Socialis* (1987); St. John Paul II, *Centisimus Annus* (1991); St. John Paul II, *Evangelium Vitae* (1995); Pope Benedict XVI, *Deus Caritas Est* (2005); Pope Benedict XVI, *Caritas in Veritate* (2009); Pope Francis, *Evangelii Gaudium* (2013); Pope Francis, *Laudato Si'* (2015).

way that it perfects the human development of students, sharpens their minds, and makes them better able to pursue theological studies."[356] The philosophy of St. Thomas Aquinas should be given the pride of place that the Church accords it.[357] Especially in the courses on the history of philosophy, there should be a significant treatment of St. Thomas's thought, along with its ancient sources and its later development. The fruitful relationship between philosophy and theology in the Christian tradition should be explored through studies in Thomistic thought as well as the thought of other great Christian theologians who were also great philosophers. These include certain Fathers of the Church, medieval Doctors, and recent Christian thinkers in the Western and Eastern traditions.[358]

THEOLOGY

285 Seminarians in the discipleship stage, build on the process they began in the propaedeutic stage and engage in courses that focus on the fundamental beliefs and practices of the Catholic faith. In particular, they should concentrate on those elements of the faith that stand as a presupposition for all forms of graduate theological study. Theology courses in the discipleship stage should study the themes contained in the *Catechism of the Catholic Church*, including courses on Catholic doctrine, liturgy and the sacraments, Catholic morality, Christian prayer, and Sacred Scripture. All seminarians should be thoroughly acquainted with the *Catechism of the Catholic Church* and its contents as a source for "a full, complete exposition of Catholic doctrine" and for "the requirements of contemporary catechetical

356 CIC, c. 251; see CCEO, c. 349 §1.

357 See *Optatam Totius*, no. 16n36; *Pastores Dabo Vobis*, no. 53; *Fides et Ratio*, nos. 43-44; CIC, c. 251; CCEO, c. 349 §1. In articulating the mind of the Fathers of the Second Vatican Council on this point, the Congregation for Catholic Education, in its document on *The Study of Philosophy in Seminaries*, observed that "the repeated recommendations of the Church about the philosophy of St. Thomas Aquinas remain fully justified and still valid. In this philosophy the first principles of natural truth are clearly and organically enunciated and harmonized with revelation. Within it also is enclosed that creative dynamism which, as biographers attest, marked the teaching of St. Thomas and which must also characterize the teaching of those who desire to follow his footsteps in a continual and renewed synthesizing of the valid conclusions received from tradition with new conquests of human thought." "Philosophy in Seminaries," *Origins* 1, no. 39 (March 16, 1972): 659.

358 See *Fides et Ratio*, no. 74.

instruction."[359] From the beginning, students should learn to relate theology to the larger mission of the Church in the public sphere. Discipleship stage study is intended as preparation for further study of theology in the configuration stage, not as a replacement for it.

286 Besides philosophical and theological studies for the intellectual dimension of discipleship stage, formation should provide seminarians with an understanding of the historical and cultural context of their faith. Men who have more extensive prior education but who might not have a full, systematic liberal arts formation should be provided a curriculum that supplies for lacunae in this area. The Catholic intellectual tradition (e.g., literature and the arts) should be a part of such a curriculum. In addition, education in rhetoric and communications as well as language study is appropriate. Latin and Greek are especially important, since competence in these languages is necessary for graduate theological studies. The study of Spanish or other pastoral languages should be included in the course of studies throughout the period of priestly formation, including the discipleship stage.

Cultural Preparation Programs

287 As stated earlier in the propaedeutic stage, international seminarians should complete an acculturation program and receive adequate instruction in the English language (if English is not their primary language), often in an ESL (English as a second language) program of study, prior to beginning the propaedeutic stage. Regional accrediting agencies require adequate proficiency in the English language as demonstrated by a TOEFL (Test of English as a Foreign Language). In addition to the study of US history and culture and of the English language, these programs may also supplement the

359 St. John Paul II, *Laetamur Magnopere* (*In which the Latin Typical Edition of the* Catechism of the Catholic Church *Is Approved and Promulgated*), in *Catechism of the Catholic Church.*

seminarians' academic and pastoral background as a preparation for the study of philosophy and theology.

288 Seminarians from the mainstream culture of the United States whose native language is English continue the intercultural competency training received during the propaedeutic stage into the discipleship stage, including the continued study of another language to meet the pastoral needs of the ecclesiastical entity.

Discipleship Stage Benchmarks

289 His study of philosophy helps the seminarian to learn the first truths of the natural order, deepens his understanding of the human person, and gives him the framework upon which to build once he concentrates on the study of theology during the configuration stage. Philosophical insights, language, and concepts will enable him to engage with the pastoral reality of the people he is called to serve. During the discipleship stage, it is important that the seminarian begins to learn how to articulate the Christian understanding of the Creator and his creation, especially the human person, and understands how this differs from the ideologies that have shaped popular conceptions of the human person, the world, and its Creator. As a result of his studies during this stage of formation, the seminarian has the ability to understand the issues surrounding the intersection of faith and modern science, as well as the ability to articulate how faith and science can support one another.[360] In addition to manifesting sufficient philosophical competence for the later study of theology in the configuration stage, the seminarian at the completion of the discipleship stage is also able to demonstrate a working knowledge of Sacred Scripture and the *Catechism of the Catholic Church*. Given the multicultural

360 Given the complex nature of the issues surrounding the human person and the intersection of faith and science, as well as other matters, seminaries will benefit from sharing ideas at a national level through organizations such as the National Association of College Seminaries and the National Association of Catholic Theological Schools.

reality of the Catholic Church in the United States of the twenty-first century, the seminarian also should possess an adequate knowledge of languages necessary for ministry; the possession of this knowledge, which was introduced in the propaedeutic stage, deepens in this and subsequent stages.

290 By the completion of the discipleship stage, the seminarian demonstrates the ability to communicate clearly in both the written and spoken word. He is also able to analyze modern and postmodern philosophy relative to basic Church teaching and the perennially valid philosophical heritage that is in harmony with it.

THE CONFIGURATION STAGE

Graduate Theology

291 Ultimately, intellectual formation in the seminary program centers on theology as a search for "an ever deeper knowledge of the divine mysteries."[361] This kind of theological study, which far exceeds a purely technical approach to "religious phenomena," unfolds in the following ways:

a. Theology in seminary intellectual formation is truly to be *fides quaerens intellectum*, faith seeking understanding.[362] This direction is not the same as the approach of religious studies or the history of religions. The seminary study of theology begins in faith and ends in faith, as should all true theological inquiry and study.

b. In a seminary or priestly formation context, the study of theology is oriented to one's own faith and also to the faith of others. In other words, the study of theology is apostolically motivated. "For the salvation of their brothers and sisters they should seek an ever deeper knowledge of the divine mysteries."[363]

---

361 *Pastores Dabo Vobis*, no. 51.
362 See *Pastores Dabo Vobis*, no. 53.
363 *Pastores Dabo Vobis*, no. 51.

c. At the same time, this study of theology, as we have already noted, enriches and expands the personal faith of the seminarian studying it.[364]

d. When theology is studied in the context of priestly formation, it cannot be detached from other human knowledge. In fact, it is to be integrated with other elements of human understanding, especially philosophy and the human sciences.[365]

e. The seminary study of theology, because it begins in faith and ends in faith, must also flow from prayer and lead to prayer.[366]

f. In a particular way, the theology studied in preparation for priestly ministry must find integration and focus in the liturgy, the celebration of the Mystery of Christ.

g. Because theology studied in light of priestly mission and ministry must be directed to a practical wisdom, it must offer a complete and unified vision of the truths of faith.[367] This wisdom and unified vision, then, can be conveyed in the priest's preaching and allow him to bring the Word of God into dialogue with the contemporary human situation.[368]

h. Because theology is rooted in the Church's faith and serves the faith of the Church, it must be studied in complete and faithful communion with the Magisterium.[369]

i. Theology studied in a seminary and destined to contribute to the mission of the Church through priestly ministry must necessarily be concerned about restoring Christian unity. Theological studies must impart an adequate grasp of the Catholic principles of ecumenism.[370] The ecumenical imperative that flows from the prayer of Christ for his flock and the renewed vision of the Second Vatican Council demand this focus.

364 See *Pastores Dabo Vobis*, no. 53.
365 See *Pastores Dabo Vobis*, no. 53.
366 See *Pastores Dabo Vobis*, no. 54.
367 See *Pastores Dabo Vobis*, no. 54.
368 See USCCB, *Fulfilled in Your Hearing: The Homily in the Sunday Assembly* (Washington, DC: USCCB, 1982), 13.
369 See *Pastores Dabo Vobis*, no. 55.
370 See Second Vatican Council, *Unitatis Redintegratio* (1964), nos. 2-4.

j. Theology's theoretical and practical dimensions in priestly mission and ministry mean that it must be rigorous in its orientation, both academically and pastorally.[371]

k. Finally, the study of theology must be an initiation into a lifelong study of the truths of faith. If the priest is to be a teacher, he must first be a student who continuously pursues an understanding of the faith to which he commits himself and invites his people.

Configuration Stage Benchmarks

292 It is expected that by the end of the configuration stage the seminarian demonstrates a well-established habit and desire to explore the Word of God and theological Tradition. He also can demonstrate the ability to uphold the truths of faith by the light of reason. He demonstrates the ability to integrate academic development with the spiritual and pastoral dimensions (e.g., the growth in knowledge about Jesus Christ deepens his friendship with Christ, his understanding of Christian anthropology influences his approaches to pastoral ministry). He also demonstrates fidelity to the Magisterium in his speech and actions. He can exercise the Ministry of the Word by proclaiming, explaining, and defending the Catholic faith.

THE VOCATIONAL SYNTHESIS STAGE

293 Intellectual formation during the vocational synthesis stage shifts to focus on ministerial application. Ongoing instruction and mentoring will help the transitional deacon to continue to grow as a preacher and teacher of the faith as he transitions into full-time ministry.[372] Liturgical and sacramental *practica* will help the man to develop ministerial competency in administering the sacraments and a proper *ars celebrandi*. Special attention can be given to prepare the deacon to be a minister of the Sacrament of Penance and help him to "translate the principles of moral theology in concrete cases, and

371 See *Pastores Dabo Vobis*, nos. 55-56.
372 See *Ratio Fundamentalis*, no. 177.

to address the questions encountered in this delicate ministry with a merciful spirit."[373] Pastoral instruction can be offered addressing various situations that will arise in the life of the priest, for example, marriage preparation and ministry to the grieving. The vocational synthesis stage may include pastoral seminars as well as sacramental *practica* that the transitional deacon attends, or these seminars and *practica* may be given in the configuration stage. Given that the transitional deacon resides full-time in a pastoral setting, virtual meeting platforms may be useful during this stage. This stage will also see the deacon establishing a habit of individual study and ongoing intellectual formation that will serve him throughout his life as a priest.

VOCATIONAL SYNTHESIS STAGE BENCHMARKS

294 As the deacon nears completion of initial formation for the priesthood, the intellectual dimension of formation in this stage focuses on demonstrating competency in pastoral theology and its application in preaching, sacramental and pastoral ministry, and liturgical praxis. Regardless of whether continued meetings or seminars are required during limited visits to the seminary, it is important that the deacon demonstrate a commitment to continued growth in intellectual formation through personal study, workshops, and conferences. It is also important that he recognize and articulate areas for his personal ongoing intellectual growth.[374]

Norms for Intellectual Formation

Propaedeutic Stage

295 In the intellectual formation of the propaedeutic stage, the seminarians should develop familiarity with Christian doctrine by studying the *Catechism of the Catholic Church*.

373 *Ratio Fundamentalis*, no. 178.
374 See CIC, c. 279; CCEO, c. 372.

296 Intellectual formation will introduce the seminarians to priestly identity in order to aid in vocational discernment.

297 The material proper to the propaedeutic stage, as expressed above, should form the bulk of the intellectual formation of this stage.

298 Part-time general education college credits are permitted but never exceed nine credit hours each semester or its equivalent.[375]

299 Classes proper to intellectual formation during the propaedeutic stage—such as courses on Scripture, catechesis, spirituality, and prayer—may be taken for credit in addition to the part-time general education credits. Courses that aid human formation, such as an introductory applied psychology course or a general physical well-being course, may also be offered for credit.

300 The formal study of philosophy is not permitted during the propaedeutic stage.

301 Care must be taken that the academic work does not interfere with the overall tenor of the propaedeutic stage and its objectives.

302 Men entering the propaedeutic stage with a college degree may still need a more general liberal arts education and hence a longer propaedeutic stage, depending on their academic background.

Discipleship Stage

303 Seminarians should have or be earning a bachelor's degree, preferably a bachelor of arts degree in philosophy, from an accredited institution. If such a degree is not available from their seminary, they may earn the degree at a college or university associated with the seminary.

---

375 The exception could be during the first two years of a three-year propaedeutic stage, where the third year would be free of academics.

304 A discipleship stage program must offer courses in philosophy and theology or provide for them at a Catholic college or university that possesses a complete curriculum of philosophical and theological studies.

305 Philosophy and theology professors should make a Profession of Faith[376] and have a mandate from the diocesan bishop or a canonical mission, dependent upon the canonical nature of the institution.

306 Sound philosophical formation requires a biennium of study, which is understood in the United States to be at least thirty semester credit hours,[377] together with the out-of-classroom work associated with each credit hour traditionally expected in US higher education. The philosophical curriculum must include the study of the history of philosophy (ancient, medieval, modern, and contemporary), logic, epistemology, metaphysics, philosophy of nature, natural theology, anthropology, and ethics. Seminaries must ensure that the philosophy is appropriate for studying Catholic theology and explore creative curricular strategies so that seminarians can grasp the relationship between philosophical insights and theological frameworks.

307 Discipleship stage should extend for at least two calendar years, regardless of previous academic or life experiences.

308 A minimum of twelve semester credit hours must be required in appropriate courses of undergraduate theology. These courses should study the themes of the *Catechism of the Catholic Church* (doctrine, liturgy and sacraments, morality, prayer) as well as Sacred Scripture.

309 The coordinator of intellectual formation and the rector should be vigilant to ensure that the philosophical and theological instruction

---

376 See CIC, c. 833, 6°.

377 See *Pastores Dabo Vobis*, no. 56; *Fides et Ratio*, no. 62.

received at a college or university is consistent with magisterial teaching and with the requirements stated in this document. Ultimately, this obligation devolves upon the diocesan bishop in view of his teaching authority.

310 Programs that utilize colleges and universities for philosophy and theological studies should carefully and consistently monitor the content and quality of their seminarians' courses as a preparation for theological studies. "Philosophical instruction must be grounded in the perennially valid philosophical heritage and also take into account philosophical investigation over the course of time."[378]

311 Special attention is to be given to classical and foreign languages. A knowledge of Latin and Greek is foundational and should be given the emphasis that the Church accords these languages.[379] Particular attention must be given to ensure that before they enter the theological study of the configuration stage, all seminarians can demonstrate that they have acquired that "knowledge of Latin which will enable them to understand and make use of so many scientific sources and of the documents of the Church," according to the insistence of the Fathers of the Second Vatican Council.[380] The study of the Spanish language and Hispanic cultures as well as other pastorally appropriate languages and cultures is recommended. In some cases, an English-language program may form an important part of the program. Since preaching is at the heart of priestly ministry, seminaries should include courses in writing and public speaking. Facility with other liturgical and spoken languages may be necessary for seminarians from the Eastern Catholic Churches.

312 Educational standards should not be so rigid or restrictive as to close the door to men who are lacking in some dimension of the required

378 CIC, c. 251; see CCEO, c. 349 §1.
379 See *Optatam Totius*, no. 13; CIC, c. 249.
380 *Optatam Totius*, no. 13.

educational background. Remedial help should be provided to such seminarians so that their academic deficiencies may be overcome. Such assistance should take the form of tutoring, academic advising, and counseling.

313 Excellence in education at the college level demands access to a strong library that offers print, nonprint, and electronic resources and that is professionally staffed, as required by accrediting agencies.

314 For men who enter the discipleship stage with a college degree, programs are encouraged to consider offering the civilly recognized bachelor in philosophy (PhB), a two-year degree program that presumes a previous bachelor's degree (preferably in the liberal arts) but does not require a liberal arts component. Such a degree requires regional accreditation.

Configuration Stage

315 At least four full years must be dedicated to graduate theological studies.[381]

316 Graduate theological studies require an appropriate and sound philosophical formation. Those requirements, identified in the norms on discipleship stage programs, are prerequisites for theological studies.

317 Philosophy and theology professors in seminaries are expected to make a Profession of Faith[382] and have a mandate from the diocesan bishop or a canonical mission, dependent upon the canonical nature of the institution.

381 See CIC, c. 250; CCEO, c. 348 §1. See also *Ratio Fundamentalis*, no. 154. The second and third models of the configuration stage are exceptions.

382 See CIC, c. 833, 6°. For seminaries with ecclesiastical faculties, see also *Veritatis Gaudium*, no. 27 §1.

318 The academic curriculum as a whole should have a discernible and coherent unity.

319 The curriculum must reflect the specialized nature of priestly formation and assist seminarians in developing a clear understanding of the ministerial priesthood.

320 Due consideration should be given to the pastoral aim of theological formation. Theological studies should be designed with the pastoral goal in view, recognizing that the pastoral character of priestly formation applies to intellectual formation as well as to the other areas of formation.[383]

321 The core should include fundamental theology: the basis of the rational procedure of all theology and thus the introduction to the study of theology.[384]

322 The various theological disciplines should recognize Sacred Scripture as foundational: as the point of departure from and as the soul of all theology.[385]

323 In Sacred Scripture, the core should include the study of the Pentateuch; the historical, prophetic, and wisdom (especially the Psalms) books of the Old Testament; the Synoptic Gospels and Acts; Pauline and Johannine literature; and the Catholic epistles.

324 The proper understanding of Sacred Scripture requires cultivation of a double awareness. On the one hand, "the books of the Old and New Testaments, whole and entire, . . . written under the inspiration

---

383 See *Pastores Dabo Vobis*, nos. 55, 57.

384 See Sacred Congregation for Catholic Education, *The Theological Formation of Future Priests* (1976), nos. 107-113.

385 See *Dei Verbum*, no. 24; *Catechism of the Catholic Church*, no. 113; CIC, c. 252 §2; CCEO, c. 350 §2; Sacred Congregation for Catholic Education, *The Theological Formation of Future Priests*, no. 79.

of the Holy Spirit, . . . have God as their author, and have been handed on as such to the Church herself." On the other hand, "to compose the sacred books, God chose certain men who . . . made full use of their own powers and faculties so that, though he acted in them and by them, it was as true authors that they consigned to writing whatever he wanted written, and no more."[386] "To interpret Scripture correctly, the reader must be attentive to what the human authors truly wanted to affirm and to what God wanted to reveal to us by their words."[387] This means "the reader must take into account the conditions of their [the human authors'] time and culture, the literary genres in use at that time, and the modes of feeling, speaking and narrating then current."[388]

325 But if *Sacred Scripture* is to be taught as Sacred Scripture and not simply as an artifact of human culture, "there is another and *no less important* principle of correct interpretation, without which Scripture would remain a dead letter: 'Sacred Scripture must be read and interpreted in the light of the same Spirit by whom it was written.'"[389] "In their work of interpretation Catholic exegetes must never forget that what they are interpreting is the *word of God.* Their common task is not finished when they have simply determined sources, defined forms or explained literary procedures. They arrive at the true goal of their work only when they have explained the meaning of the biblical text as God's word for today."[390] This requires (1) attention to "the content and unity of the whole Scripture"; (2) reading of Sacred Scripture within "the living Tradition of the whole Church"; and (3) attention to the "analogy of faith."[391] Otherwise, the study of Sacred Scripture cannot serve as the "soul of sacred theology,"[392] and a dichotomy will arise between the study

386 *Dei Verbum*, no. 11.
387 *Catechism of the Catholic Church*, no. 109. See *Dei Verbum*, no. 12.
388 *Catechism of the Catholic Church*, no. 110.
389 *Catechism of the Catholic Church*, no. 111, emphasis added; see *Dei Verbum*, no. 12.
390 Pontifical Biblical Commission, *The Interpretation of the Bible in the Church* (1993), III.C.1.
391 *Catechism of the Catholic Church*, nos. 112-114. See *Dei Verbum*, no. 12.
392 *Dei Verbum*, no. 24.

of Sacred Scripture and the rest of theology. "This dichotomy can create confusion and a lack of stability in the intellectual formation of candidates for ecclesial ministries."[393]

326 The study of Sacred Scripture and its interpretation should take into account the preparation of seminarians for the tasks of preaching homilies and applying Sacred Scripture to the lives of the Christian faithful.[394]

327 Patristic studies constitute an essential part of theological studies. Theology should draw from the works of the Fathers of the Church because of their lasting value within the living Tradition of the Church. The core should include patrology (an overview of the life and writings of the Fathers of the Church) and patristics (an overview of the theological thought of the Fathers of the Church).[395]

328 In dogmatic theology, the core must include theology of the Blessed Trinity, Christology, pneumatology, creation, the Fall and the nature of sin, redemption, grace and the human person, ecclesiology, sacraments, eschatology, Mariology,[396] and missiology.[397] A separate course on Holy Orders, with a thorough study of the nature and mission of the ministerial priesthood including a history and theology of celibacy, is required.[398]

329 The Church enjoins pastors "to neglect nothing with a view to a well-organized and well-oriented catechetical effort"; and since "all pastors have the duty to provide" them, evangelization and catechesis should

393 *Verbum Domini*, no. 35.

394 Because "in the sacred books the Father who is in heaven comes lovingly to meet his children, and talks with them," courses in Sacred Scripture must equip seminarians to identify those "divinely revealed realities, which are contained and presented" therein (*Dei Verbum*, nos. 21, 11), so that they can share these riches with those whom they serve.

395 See Congregation for Catholic Education, *Instruction on the Study of the Fathers of the Church in the Formation of Priests* (1989); see also *Optatam Totius*, no. 16.

396 See Congregation for Catholic Education, *The Virgin Mary in Intellectual and Spiritual Formation* (1988).

397 Missiology may be treated as a separate component or integrated into ecclesiology; it must form an integral part of every treatment of evangelization. See *Ratio Fundamentalis*, no. 171.

398 See *Sacramentum Caritatis*, no. 24.

have a prominent place in the seminary curriculum.[399] A sound study of the content and methods of catechesis not only prepares the seminarian for his task as a minister of the Word but also provides the possibility of a synthetic moment in the curriculum when an integrated unity can be brought to his years of theological study.[400]

330 In moral theology, the core must include fundamental moral theology, health care ethics, sexual morality, and social doctrine.

331 Moral theology should be taught in a way that draws deeply from Sacred Scripture, Tradition, and the Magisterium, in particular *Veritatis Splendor*. The Christian moral life should be presented in light of the new law of the grace of the Holy Spirit, who transforms the human person, gives him a new heart, and enables him to follow the example of Christ and live according to the moral law. Moral theology should treat the path to happiness which consists in following the inspirations and the Gifts of the Holy Spirit and living according to the Beatitudes, the virtues, and the moral law, including absolute moral norms.

Therefore, moral theology should illustrate that the ultimate end of graced human acts is the beatitude to which God calls us: a participation in the life of the Blessed Trinity. The inseparable connections among moral theology, Sacred Scripture, spiritual theology, theological anthropology, and dogmatic theology should be evident, with particular attention paid to the synthesis of the Christian moral life in the writings of St. Thomas Aquinas. Moreover, an understanding of the moral sense of Sacred Scripture should be developed[401] to prepare future priests for preaching on Christian morality. The preparation of future priests to be ministers of the Sacrament of Penance should also be kept in mind in the teaching of moral theology. Finally, the contribution of the natural and human sciences to moral theology should be considered.

399 St. John Paul II, *Catechesi Tradendae* (*On Catechesis in Our Time*) (Washington, DC: USCCB, 1979), no. 64.
400 See *Optatam Totius*, no. 19; CIC, cc. 254, 256; CCEO, c. 352 §§2-3.
401 See *Catechism of the Catholic Church*, nos. 115-118.

332 It is vital that the intellectual dimension in teaching moral theology be integrated with the pastoral dimension in applying moral theology to the lives of the People of God. Pastoral ministry requires more than the presentation of moral principles. Helping seminarians understand this is critical to formation in pastoral charity. Priests are called upon to assist the faithful in the formation of a sound moral conscience in accord with Sacred Scripture, Tradition, and magisterial teaching. This formation will enable each person to grow in authentic prudence and virtuous Christian acts in the midst of difficult and at times oppressive circumstances. The formation of priests in moral theology should intersect with formation in compassionate listening and in thoughtful counseling, with the pastoral goal of gently but consistently fostering the love of God and neighbor. This is especially important in the areas of sexuality and family life.

333 The importance of a clear grasp of the principles of health care ethics cannot be overestimated for the future priest in the contemporary culture. Special attention during his preparation should be given to the fundamental respect for human life from conception to natural death and to the moral evils of and pastoral means of addressing contraception, in vitro fertilization, abortion, and euthanasia.

334 The teaching of sexual morality must be thorough and unambiguous in its presentation of the authentic teaching of the Church in sexual moral matters—presuming a mature biological and basic social scientific understanding of human sexuality. Seminarians must be prepared to engage the contemporary world in dialogue regarding the complex issues of sexual morality and gender ideology. This is a matter of special import since the seminarian's formation in celibate chastity includes the intellectual assent to, and embrace of, the Church's moral teachings in all matters of sexuality.

335 The social doctrine of the Church must be presented in its entirety with appropriate principles of reflection, criteria for judgment, and norms for pastoral practice. The systematic study of the social encyclicals of the popes is especially recommended.[402]

336 Of particular importance today is the need for awareness of the ecological crisis facing the world. Seminarians must be familiar with Church teaching on the subject and be encouraged to experience an ecological conversion, "whereby the effects of their encounter with Jesus Christ become evident in their relationship with the world around them. Living our vocation to be protectors of God's handiwork is essential to a life of virtue; it is not an optional or a secondary aspect of our Christian experience."[403]

337 Adequate instruction must be given in professional ethics appropriate to priesthood and priestly ministry. In the process of this instruction, "seminarians must receive a careful training in the administration of goods, to be carried out according to canonical norms, soberly, with detachment and moral transparency, along with the necessary skill."[404]

338 In historical studies, the core should include courses on the history of the Universal Church and the history of the Catholic Church in the United States, taught in a way that reflects the Church's multicultural origins and ecumenical context. Among historical studies, the study of patristics and the lives of the saints are of special importance.

339 In Canon Law, the core must include a general introduction to Canon Law and to the Canon Law of individual sacraments, including but

402 See Congregation for Catholic Education, *Guidelines for the Study and Teaching of the Church's Social Doctrine in the Formation of Priests* (1988), *www.humandevelopment.va/content/dam/sviluppoumano/pubblicazioni-documenti/archivio/dottrina-sociale-della-chiesa/orientamenti/ODSI_ENG.pdf.* See also *Ratio Fundamentalis*, no. 172.
403 *Laudato Si'*, no. 217. See *Ratio Fundamentalis*, no. 172.
404 *Ratio Fundamentalis*, no. 180.

not limited to the Sacrament of Matrimony. Additional courses in Canon Law, particularly on books II ("The People of God"), V ("The Temporal Goods of the Church"), and VI ("Penal Sanctions in the Church") of the *Code of Canon Law* would assist seminarians in preparing for their pastoral ministry. There should also be a general introduction to the *Code of Canons of the Eastern Churches*, with emphasis on title II (cc. 27-41) regarding Churches *sui iuris* and rites and on title XVI, chap. 7 (cc. 776-866) on marriage, especially the divergences between the Latin and Eastern Codes in sacramental discipline.[405] Seminarians should learn how to make appropriate referrals for issues that are beyond their competence.

340 Studies in spiritual theology and spiritual direction are to be included. Spiritual theology includes studies in the Catholic spiritual Tradition, provides practical directives for the Christian call to perfection, and proposes principles of discernment. This study should also explore the spirituality of various vocations, especially the priesthood and consecrated life.[406] Spiritual direction teaches the art of fostering the spiritual life of those entrusted to one's care: "In view of the pastoral care of the faithful, formation in the discernment of spirits and in spiritual direction should receive attention as an integral part of priestly ministry."[407]

341 In liturgy, the core should include studies in the theological, historical, spiritual, pastoral, and juridical aspects of liturgy.[408]

342 Seminarians must learn to celebrate the Church's sacred rites according to the mind of the Church, without addition or subtraction. Liturgical practica should include the celebration of the Eucharist and the

405 See CIC, c. 256 §1; CCEO, c. 352 §§2-3; Congregation for Catholic Education, *On the Teaching of Canon Law to Those Preparing to Be Priests* (1975).
406 See *Ratio Fundamentalis*, no. 169.
407 *Ratio Fundamentalis*, no. 178.
408 See Congregation for Catholic Education, *Instruction on Liturgical Formation in Seminaries* (1979).

other sacraments, with particular attention given to the practicum for the Sacrament of Penance. Seminarians should be introduced to the official liturgical books used by the clergy and to the Church's directives for music, art, and architecture.[409] Knowledge of sacred art and music should be integrated into liturgical formations so that it "will contribute to the overall formation of seminarians, and provide them with another resource in view of evangelization and pastoral endeavor."[410]

343 Homiletics should occupy a prominent place in the core curriculum and should be integrated into the entire course of studies. In addition to the principles of biblical interpretation, catechesis, and communications theory, seminarians should also learn the practical skills needed to communicate the Gospel as proclaimed by the Church in an effective and appropriate manner. Seminarians should be taught that "through the course of the liturgical year the homily sets forth the mysteries of faith and the standards of the Christian life on the basis of the sacred text."[411] While the homily is reserved to a priest or deacon,[412] seminarians should be afforded opportunities to preach outside of Mass and receive proper assessment. Examples of these opportunities could include seminarians giving reflections in their pastoral assignments to parish groups like youth groups or fraternal organizations, as well as offering meditations at communal devotions.[413] Where appropriate, seminarians should be able to demonstrate a capacity for bilingual preaching.

344 The core curriculum should include an introductory course in ecumenism that treats of the Catholic Church's commitment to

409 See *Ecclesia de Eucharistia*, no. 5; *General Instruction of the Roman Missal*, nos. 5-6.
410 *Ratio Fundamentalis*, no. 181.
411 *Praenotanda* of the *Lectionary for the Mass* (1981), no. 24.
412 CIC, c. 767 §1; CCEO, c. 614 §4. The 1997 interdicastery document *Instruction on Certain Questions Regarding the Collaboration of the Non-Ordained Faithful in the Sacred Ministry of Priest*, §1, states, "The practice, on some occasions, of entrusting the preaching of the homily to seminarians or theology students who are not clerics is not permitted. Indeed, the homily should not be regarded as a training for some future ministry" (*www.vatican.va/roman_curia/pontifical_councils/laity/documents/rc_con_interdic_doc_15081997_en.html*).
413 See CIC, c. 766; USCCB, "Complementary Norms, Canon 766 - Lay Preaching" (2002).

the principles of ecumenism, the fundamental role of ecumenical dialogue, and current ecumenical issues. In addition, ecumenism should be fully integrated into other courses, thus permeating the theological curriculum. Issues concerning interreligious dialogue should also be discussed.[414] Seminarians should learn about the religious traditions present in the United States.

345 Studies in pastoral theology are required, should include treatment of the principles and criteria for pastoral action, and should provide for theological reflection where seminarians are involved in supervised pastoral placements.[415] Pastoral studies should include training in pastoral counseling, in which seminarians are to learn how to address concerns brought to them by parishioners for whom they can reasonably offer counsel and how to make appropriate referrals for issues beyond their competence.

346 Due emphasis should be given in the various theological disciplines to the topics of consecrated life,[416] marriage, and the family. There should be interdisciplinary cooperation, and the curriculum should be organized so that these topics become an important dimension of pastoral and intellectual formation.[417]

347 Although various theological schools exist within the Catholic Tradition, in accord with Church teaching, the significance of St. Thomas Aquinas as the model and guide for study and research in theology must be recognized.[418]

---

414 See Pontifical Council for Promoting Christian Unity, *Directory for the Application of Principles and Norms of Ecumenism* (1993). See also Second Vatican Council, *Unitatis Redintegratio* and *Nostra Aetate* (1965); St. John Paul II, *Ut Unum Sint*; Pontifical Council for Promoting Christian Unity, *The Ecumenical Dimension of the Formation of Those Engaged in Pastoral Work* (1997) and *"The Gifts and the Calling of God Are Irrevocable": Rom 11:29* (2015); and Pontifical Council for Interreligious Dialogue, *Dialogue in Truth and Charity: Pastoral Orientations for Interreligious Dialogue* (2014).

415 See *Pastores Dabo Vobis*, no. 57; Sacred Congregation for Catholic Education, *The Theological Formation of Future Priests*, nos. 102-106.

416 See *Ratio Fundamentalis*, no. 169.

417 See Congregation for Catholic Education, *Directives on the Formation of Seminarians Concerning Problems Related to Marriage and the Family* (1995).

418 See *Optatam Totius*, no. 16n36; CIC, c. 252 §3.

348 Throughout the academic curriculum, questions of theological methodology should be emphasized so that seminarians learn to evaluate the strengths and limitations of various theological viewpoints in light of the Magisterium of the Church.

349 All methodologies employed must be clear on the distinction and relation between truths revealed by God and contained in the Deposit of Faith and their theological mode of expression.[419]

350 The normative function of the Magisterium must be presented as Christ's gift to his Church: the vital, integral, and authoritative voice in the theological enterprise.

351 Courses of theology, ecclesiology, spirituality, and history should include the development and nature of the Eastern Churches.[420]

352 Studies in the beliefs and practices of other Churches, ecclesial communities, or religions may be profitably taught by members of those Churches or religions after seminarians have completed the regular course studies on ecclesiology and the Catholic principles on ecumenism, and with respect for the rule that in seminary studies the professors of the doctrinal courses should be Catholics.[421] The prescriptions of the *Directory for the Application of Principles and Norms on Ecumenism* (nos. 70-81, 192-95) and *The Ecumenical Dimension in the Formation of Those Engaged in Pastoral Work* are to be followed.

353 The expansion of communications technology and social media is a phenomenon that must be taken into account in the intellectual formation of seminarians. "Considering the ample attention given

419 See International Theological Commission, *On the Interpretation of Dogmas* (1989).
420 See CCEO, c. 41; Congregation for Catholic Education, *Circular Letter Concerning Studies of the Oriental Churches* (1987).
421 See Pontifical Council for Promoting Christian Unity, *Directory for the Application of Principles and Norms on Ecumenism*.

by the Magisterium to the theme of social communications, and the promising area of evangelization found in the 'new media,' Seminaries must develop a specific awareness in seminarians in this regard."[422]

354 Theological formation in seminaries must clearly respect traditional doctrinal formulations of the faith while recognizing contemporary modes of theological expression and explanation that accord with the doctrine of the faith. Contemporary expressions are always to be presented with due deference for the Tradition and in continuity with it.[423]

355 Theological education for the priesthood should resist any tendency to reduce theology to a merely historical, sociological investigation or to a comparative study of religions.

356 The entire academic program should be taught in such a way that it makes seminarians aware that they have a responsibility to continue their theological and pastoral education after ordination.[424]

357 The theological curriculum, in both its planning and its execution, should address the unique needs of a multicultural society, which entails not only the study of the Spanish language and Hispanic cultures, but also direction regarding such matters as approved Marian apparitions and the lives of those Americans who have been canonized or beatified.[425] Seminaries should offer resources for attaining proficiency in pastorally appropriate languages.[426]

---

422 *Ratio Fundamentalis*, no. 182; see CIC, c. 666.

423 Pope Benedict XVI provides a helpful principle regarding contemporary expressions of the faith: "On the one hand, there is an interpretation that I would call 'a hermeneutic of discontinuity and rupture'; it has frequently availed itself of the sympathies of the mass media, and also one trend of modern theology. On the other, there is the 'hermeneutic of reform,' of renewal in the continuity of the one subject-Church which the Lord has given to us. She is a subject which increases in time and develops, yet always remaining the same, the one subject of the journeying People of God." Address to the Roman Curia Offering Them Christmas Greetings, December 22, 2005, *www.vatican.va/content/benedict-xvi/en/speeches/2005/december/documents/hf_ben_xvi_spe_20051222_roman-curia.html*.

424 See *Ratio Fundamentalis*, no. 56.

425 See *Ratio Fundamentalis*, no. 157.

426 See USCCB, *Encuentro and Mission: A Renewed Pastoral Framework for Hispanic Ministry* (Washington, DC: USCCB, 2002), 55.

358 Throughout the curriculum, the biblical, theological, ethical, and historical foundations of the Church's teaching on social justice should be included.[427]

359 Seminarians must receive an introduction to the principles, methods, and skills of catechesis and teaching.[428] Teaching opportunities may be offered as a part of field education and pastoral placements. In addition, seminarians should be given a doctrinal understanding of popular piety to teach them "to distinguish what belongs to the inculturation of the Gospel and constitutes a real treasure for the Church."[429]

360 In the United States, the first professional degree, a master of divinity, is the recognized standard for preparation of students for ordained ministry across the broad spectrum of institutions of graduate theological education. Its curriculum incorporates the requirements of the *Program of Priestly Formation*. Seminaries in the United States may offer a master of arts degree in theology to provide a deeper understanding of the theological disciplines for general educational purposes or for further graduate study. In addition, seminaries may also offer the ecclesiastical degrees of bachelor of sacred theology (STB) and the licentiate in sacred theology (STL) either by affiliating with an ecclesiastical faculty or by special arrangement with the Congregation for Catholic Education.

361 Seminaries should have degree programs certified by appropriate accrediting agencies. Seminarians should not be excused from pursuing such degrees except for serious reasons. A seminarian is normally expected to obtain the master of divinity and/or the STB degree prior to ordination.

---

427 See *Compendium of the Social Doctrine of the Church*.
428 See CIC, cc. 528, 773, 776-777.
429 *Ratio Fundamentalis*, no. 179.

362 As an essential resource for seminarians' life of study and reflection, the library collection of books and periodicals should be carefully maintained and appropriately expanded. Excellence in education at the graduate level demands access to a strong, professionally staffed library with print, nonprint, and electronic resources, as required by accrediting agencies.

363 Contemporary pedagogical methods that incorporate technological advances should be encouraged.

364 Diocesan bishops and major superiors should be encouraged to designate seminarians who complete their basic program with honors for further study after sufficient pastoral experience.

Vocational Synthesis Stage

365 The intellectual dimension of the vocational synthesis stage should focus on the practical application of theology needed for sacramental and pastoral ministry as well as preaching and teaching. The deacon will have completed his formal theological study and turned a greater focus to ministerial practice. Nevertheless, he is to cultivate the practice of ongoing study in theology and other vital disciplines.

Pastoral Dimension

366 All four dimensions of formation are interwoven and go forward concurrently. Still, in a certain sense, pastoral formation is the culmination of the entire formation process. "The whole formation imparted to candidates for the priesthood aims at preparing them to enter into communion with the charity of Christ the good shepherd";[430] therefore "priestly formation must be permeated by a pastoral spirit."[431]

367 The goal of pastoral formation is to form shepherds of God's People; this goal requires men who are not self-centered, aloof, judgmental, or self-imposing but instead are characterized by a "serene openness" and capable of listening and collaboration. True shepherds must have a desire to understand the hearts of others and engage in attentive accompaniment.[432]

368 In virtue of the sacramental character of Holy Orders, a priest is able to stand and act in the community in the name and person of Jesus Christ, Head and Shepherd of the Church. The fruitfulness of this sacramental character requires the personal and pastoral formation of the priest, who appropriates "the mind of Christ" and effectively communicates the mysteries of faith through his human personality as a bridge, through his personal witness of faith rooted in his spiritual life, and through his knowledge of faith. These dimensions of formation converge in pastoral formation.

369 The basic principle of pastoral formation is enunciated in *Pastores Dabo Vobis*: "The whole training of the students should have as its

430 *Pastores Dabo Vobis*, no. 57.
431 *Ratio Fundamentalis*, no. 119.
432 See *Ratio Fundamentalis*, no. 120. "The pastoral care of the faithful demands that the priest have a solid formation and interior maturity." *Ratio Fundamentalis*, no. 41.

object to make them true shepherds of souls after the example of our Lord Jesus Christ, teacher, priest, and shepherd."[433] To be a true "shepherd of souls" means to stand with and for Christ in the community, the Christ who teaches, sanctifies, and guides or leads the community. The grace to be a shepherd comes with ordination. That grace, however, calls for the priest's personal commitment to develop the knowledge and skills to teach and preach well, to celebrate the sacraments both properly and prayerfully, and to respond to people's needs as well as to take initiatives in the community that holy servant leadership requires. Developing this knowledge and these skills while still in the initial stages of formation enables him as a priest to assume the role of a shepherd, who learns to recognize God at work in the lives of his flock and who, ever present to them as a "man of communion," directs the flock to Christ.[434]

370 The aim of pastoral formation—the formation of a "true shepherd" who teaches, sanctifies, and governs or leads—implies that such formation must include a number of essential elements:

a. *Proclamation of the Word*: Pastoral formation needs to emphasize the proclamation of God's Word, which indeed is the first task of the priest.[435] This proclamation is aimed at the spiritual nourishment of the people and the conversion of sinners and is rooted in the seminarian's or preacher's ability to listen deeply to the lived experiences and realities of the faithful. This listening is followed by the preacher's ability to interpret those lived experiences in the light of Sacred Scripture and the Church's Tradition.[436]

Understanding this intersection of God's Word and human experiences, the seminarian as preacher initiates a lifelong mission

433 *Pastores Dabo Vobis*, no. 57, citing *Optatam Totius*, no. 4.

434 *Ratio Fundamentalis*, no. 119.

435 See *Presbyterorum Ordinis*, no. 4.

436 See USCCB, *Fulfilled in Your Hearing*, 20; USCCB Committee on CCLV, *Preaching the Mystery of Faith*. See also St. John Paul II, letter to Archbishop John L. May, president of the National Conference of Catholic Bishops, August 8, 1987; *Notes on the Correct Way to Present Jews and Judaism in Preaching and Catechesis in the Roman Catholic Church* (1985); *We Remember: A Reflection on the Shoah* (1998).

and ministry of bringing God's Word to the world through preaching and teaching. This requires that the seminarian couple the deepest convictions of faith with the development of his communication skills, so that God's Word may be effectively expressed.

b. *The sacramental dimension*: The celebration of the sacraments is central to the priest's ministry. Although the seminarian cannot celebrate the sacraments as a priest does, he can accompany priests who do, and he can prepare those who participate in them. In this way, he begins to have a sense of what his sacramental ministry will entail. He will come to appreciate the sacraments as part of his future public ministry for the salvation of souls and understand more clearly how the Church's sacraments, especially Penance and the Eucharist, nourish and sustain God's people.

c. *Ecclesial formation*: All pastoral formation, on the universal, diocesan, and parochial levels, must be profoundly ecclesial and missionary in nature. Notwithstanding the specific situation of seminarians of an institute of consecrated life or society of apostolic life, diocesan seminarians must be familiarized with the local Church that they will serve and especially with the priests, with whom they will be co-workers with the bishop.

This dimension of pastoral formation means not only absorbing information about the local Church and presbyterate but, more importantly, cultivating bonds of affective communion and learning how to be at home in the place where one will serve and with the priests with whom one will serve.[437] Seminarians should see their future priestly assignments as something wider than their own preference and choice and as a sharing in a far wider vision of the needs of the local Church. At the same time, seminarians must

437 "The example of priests who have preceded the candidates into the priesthood will be a great help and incentive. This will include the elderly, the pastors who lead the Diocese, as well as the emeritus Bishops. It is a matter of making the 'pastoral tradition' of the local Church known and appreciated, the better to ease their future entry into pastoral life, for it is there that they will be incardinated and exercise the ministry." *Ratio Fundamentalis*, no. 123.

understand that their hearts and minds should bear a concern for the Universal Church as well.[438]

Lastly, it is necessary that all priests have the heart of missionaries.[439] The Church is truest to her identity when she is an evangelizing Church, because the very nature of the Church is missionary.[440] Seminarians must be taught the concern for all Churches and people and should be given an opportunity to become acquainted with the work of the Pontifical Mission Societies, the Missionary Congregations of Religious, the home missions, and the missionary tradition over the centuries. An exposure to the Church's missionary work during the years of formation can be beneficial to the seminarian, his discernment, and his future ministry.

d. *The community dimension*: Pastoral formation must initiate seminarians to the care, guidance, and leadership that are extended to a community. The pastor is to be a man of communion and the shepherd of a flock. In the context of individualism in the United States, the concern is that "pastoral formation" and "pastoral care" might otherwise be limited to one-to-one contact.

Pastoral ministry is primarily directed to a community and then to individuals within that community. Seminarians need to learn how to integrate and make available in service to God's People all the formation they have received from all dimensions. This means the acquisition of certain skills, for example, an ability to communicate the mysteries of faith in clear and readily comprehensible language[441] using media and technology appropriate to the social context.

At the same time, pastoral formation means more than acquiring skills. It signifies a level of personal development, fitting for a priest who acts in the person of Jesus Christ, Head and Shepherd, Servant

---

438 "Seminarians ought to be moved by an authentically Catholic spirit. While loving their own Diocese sincerely, they ought to be open to placing themselves at the service of the Universal Church or of other particular Churches." *Ratio Fundamentalis*, no. 123. See CIC, c. 257 §1; CCEO, c. 352 §3.

439 See St. John Paul II, *Redemptoris Missio*, no. 67.

440 See Second Vatican Council, *Ad Gentes Divinitus* (*Decree on the Church's Mission Activity*), in Austin Flannery, ed., *Vatican Council II: Volume 1: The Conciliar and Post Conciliar Documents*, new rev. ed. (Collegeville, MN: Liturgical Press, 1996), no. 2; *Evangelii Gaudium*, no. 19.

441 See CIC, c. 255; CCEO, c. 352 §2.

and Spouse. Effective ministry means, for example, the cultivation of a flexibility of spirit that enables the priest to relate to people across a number of different cultures and theological and ecclesial outlooks. Formators must help the seminarian put on both the mind and heart of Christ, the Good Shepherd,[442] including exposing him to cultural and linguistic diversity. This exposure enables him to more fully welcome newcomers to the culturally rich society in which we live, while at the same time encouraging these newcomers to maintain the richness of their own cultural identity.[443]

e. *Collaboration with others*: Pastoral formation must give the seminarian the experience of working with various leaders within the Church, such as permanent deacons, the laity, and those in the state of consecrated life, so as to prepare him for fruitful collaboration with others as a priest.[444]

f. *Catholic education*: Pastoral formation must help seminarians develop an awareness and appreciation of the necessity of the education and formation of our young people. Catholic schools, parochial religious education, and youth ministry are all important means of evangelization and catechesis.

g. *A personal synthesis for practical use*: Another way of viewing pastoral formation is to see it as a process linking the elements of human, spiritual, and intellectual formation in such a way that they can be put to practical use for others, especially in a parish context.[445] In a parish internship experience, for example, the seminarian draws on the experience before him in the parish and asks how his human, spiritual, and intellectual formation makes a difference. With due attention to the discipline of the Church, preaching might be one instance of a theoretical, personal, and practical synthesis. Other examples include evangelization, catechesis, and participation in the

442 See *Pastores Dabo Vobis*, no. 58.
443 Useful resources for formation in cultural competency are noted in the section on the propaedeutic stage.
444 See *Ratio Fundamentalis*, no. 119.
445 See *Pastores Dabo Vobis*, no. 58.

Church's social justice ministry. In these and other ways, he revisits his formation and views it through the lens of practice, application, and impact.[446]

h. *An initiation to various practical, pastoral experiences, especially in parishes*: It is important not to sacrifice human, spiritual, and intellectual formation for practical experience. Still, it is essential to cultivate pastoral formation and to enhance and integrate the other dimensions of formation so that the seminarian has opportunities to experience pastoral life firsthand.[447]

Seminaries must initiate seminarians into pastoral experiences and pastoral reflection in a variety of ways including concurrent field placements and internships. In the vocational synthesis stage, reflection with the pastoral team at his assignment and with his formators will help the newly ordained deacon to synthesize and strengthen the integration of all he has experienced in formation.

Whatever the setting, it is necessary that it facilitates learning. It is also necessary that there be a guide, mentor, or teacher who accompanies the seminarian and helps him to learn from the experience. In addition, there must be a skilled priest supervisor who helps the seminarian enter into the specifically priestly dimension of the ministry.[448]

In these experiences, the seminarian first enters the scene as an observer, then raises questions to understand what is happening, and finally relates it to his other formation. He should then practice or try to do what the situation requires. After that, he can profit from supervision that helps him to assess what happened and gives him feedback.

A process of theological reflection follows that identifies the faith assumptions and convictions underlying both the situation and the ministerial response. Theological reflection thus provides an

446 The goal is "to help the seminarian to acquire the inner freedom to live the apostolate as service, able to see the work of God in the hearts and lives of the people." *Ratio Fundamentalis*, no. 119.
447 See *Pastores Dabo Vobis*, no. 58; CCEO, c. 353.
448 See CIC, c. 258.

opportunity for personal synthesis, the clarification of motivations, and the development of directions for life and ministry.

And the final step, of course, is in fact to return to the ministry or pastoral situation, but now with more knowledge and ability and a better inner sense of direction because of an enriched spiritual life and a more deeply grounded sense of priestly identity. It is the responsibility of the diocesan bishop, the major superior, and the rectors to ensure that the Catholic, sacramental dimension of pastoral care is integral to all such programs in which seminarians participate.

i. *Cultural sensitivity*: Pastoral formation must flow from and move toward an appreciation of the multifaceted reality of the Church.[449] In the United States, this means a genuine appreciation of the diversity that marks the Catholic Church as well as the diversity that typifies this society generally. Seminarians need exposure to the many cultures and languages that belong to the Catholic Church in the United States. They should know how to welcome migrants and refugees pastorally, liturgically, and culturally. Simultaneously, they should assist newcomers to adapt themselves into the mainstream without losing their own identity.[450] Seminaries that serve ecclesiastical entities that have a constant flux of immigrants should ensure that seminarians take courses and receive pastoral experience that can help them to hone applicable ministerial skills to serve immigrants.

j. *Religious pluralism*: Seminarians also need to know, appreciate, and learn how to work within the ecumenical and interfaith context that forms a backdrop for life in the United States and for the Catholic Church in this nation.

k. *The poor*: If seminarians are to be formed after the model of Jesus, the Good Shepherd, who came "to bring glad tidings to the poor," then they must have sustained contact with those who are privileged in God's eyes—the poor, the marginalized, the sick,

449 See *Pastores Dabo Vobis*, no. 59.

450 See Pontifical Council for the Pastoral Care of Migrants and Itinerant People, *Erga Migrantes* (*Instruction on the Love of Christ Towards Migrants*, 2004). The propaedeutic stage section lists resources for formation in cultural sensitivity and intercultural competency.

and the suffering. In the course of these encounters, they learn to cultivate a preferential option for the poor. They also need to become aware of the social contexts and structures that can breed injustice as well as ways of promoting more just contexts and structures.

l. *Ministry to all walks of life*: As much as possible, pastoral assignments are to give seminarians experience with all age groups in the Church; it is important they are taught to bring the mercy and love of God to everyone. In particular, the sick, the elderly, the disabled, those who live in isolation (such as migrants), and prisoners deserve particular attention.[451] The social sciences serve pastoral theology by assisting future priests in grasping the context of ministry in all walks of life.

m. *Leadership development*: Pastoral formation means that seminarians learn how to take spiritual initiatives and direct a community into action or movement. That leadership also includes a dimension of practical administration. The pastoral formation program should provide opportunities for seminarians to acquire the basic administrative skills necessary for effective pastoral leadership, recognizing that programs of continuing education and ongoing formation will be necessary to equip newly ordained priests to assume future responsibilities as pastors.

Additional leadership skills include an ability to manage the physical and financial resources of the parish, including educating parishioners about the Gospel value of stewardship, supervising staff and volunteers, making effective use of pastoral and finance councils, and organizing parochial life effectively to achieve the goals of evangelization. It is important to recognize that lay persons, especially those working at diocesan offices, bring an essential expertise. Further, the experience of seasoned pastors is invaluable, as is the development of working relationships between future priests and diocesan officials.

451 See *Ratio Fundamentalis*, no. 124.

n. *Professional standards*: Every seminarian must become capable of practicing and promoting the professional standards of ministerial behavior that are expected of all Church employees and volunteers, including ministerial codes of conduct and policies regarding conflict of interest, financial transparency, appropriate boundaries, and the use of social media.

o. *The cultivation of personal qualities*: In the current situation in the United States, parish life is blessed with many people who serve: permanent deacons, consecrated men and women, professional lay ministers, volunteers, and members of parish and diocesan consultative bodies. To direct others and to work well with them, priests need a number of personal qualities. A seminarian who aspires to serve as a priest needs to cultivate these qualities in the process of pastoral formation. They include a sense of responsibility for initiating and completing tasks, time management abilities, a spirit of collaboration with others, an ability to facilitate resolution of conflicts, a flexibility of spirit that can make adjustments for new and unexpected circumstances, an availability to those who serve and those who are served, and finally zeal—or the ardent desire to bring all people closer to the Lord.

371 Pastoral formation depends in great measure on the quality of supervision. To serve as a supervisor of seminarians calls for experience, competence, and generosity. Priests and others who serve as supervisors, mentors, and professors are an extension of the seminary. It is important that this identification with priestly formation become part of the mindset of pastoral staffs who serve to initiate seminarians to pastoral life. When onsite pastoral formation is seen as an integral part of priestly formation, then pastoral staffs must accept a special responsibility in the name of the Church for the direction and help they provide to seminarians. These priests and those associated with them must have certain qualities that include loyal commitment to priestly formation, patience, honesty, an almost instinctive way of thinking theologically in pastoral situations, and a habit of prayer that permeates their ministry.

372 Clearly, pastoral formation not only connects with the other three dimensions of priestly formation but, in itself, provides a goal that integrates the other dimensions. Human formation enables priests to be bridges to communicate Jesus Christ, a pastoral function. Spiritual formation enables priests to persevere in and give depth to their ministry. Intellectual formation provides criteria and content to ensure that pastoral efforts are directed correctly, properly, and effectively.

PROPAEDEUTIC STAGE BENCHMARKS

373 Seminarians in the propaedeutic stage should develop "the dynamic of self-giving through experiences in the parish setting and charitable works."[452] Hands-on experiences that include contact with the poor are appropriate at this stage. Benchmarks in the pastoral dimension include an awareness of the pastoral situation of the local community or ecclesiastical entity, as well as an awareness of the multicultural reality of the Church in the United States and the nature of the Universal Church. Priests serving in the United States, regardless of their cultural background, often serve in a multicultural setting. Working toward cultural competency, including language competency, to meet pastoral needs in his diocese should be part of the formation a seminarian receives during the propaedeutic stage, so as to lay a solid foundation for continued formation in cultural competency in later stages.[453] Pastoral charity is at the heart of the Church and the priesthood; so demonstrating a genuine concern for

452 *Ratio Fundamentalis*, no. 59.

453 Useful resources for formation in cultural competency include USCCB Committee on Cultural Diversity in the Church, *Open Wide Our Hearts: The Enduring Call to Love—A Pastoral Letter Against Racism* (Washington, DC: USCCB, 2018); USCCB Subcommittee on Asian and Pacific Island Affairs, under the direction of the USCCB Committee on Cultural Diversity in the Church, *Encountering Christ in Harmony: A Pastoral Response to Our Asian and Pacific Island Brothers and Sisters* (Washington, DC: USCCB, 2018); USCCB Committee on Cultural Diversity in the Church, *Building Intercultural Competence for Ministers* (Washington, DC: USCCB, 2014); USCCB Committee on Cultural Diversity in the Church, *Best Practices for Shared Parishes: So That They May All Be One* (Washington, DC: USCCB, 2013).

others, a spirit of generosity, and a developing habit of self-donation are also necessary benchmarks to be achieved prior to the seminarian's acceptance into the discipleship stage.

DISCIPLESHIP STAGE BENCHMARKS

374 "As the Second Vatican Council reminds us, the nature and mission of priests must be understood within the Church, the People of God, the Body of Christ, the Temple of the Holy Spirit, for the service of which they consecrate their lives."[454] The foundation in pastoral knowledge, pastoral skills, and pastoral charity, which is laid during the discipleship stage, will enable the seminarian in the following stages to continue to develop the skills necessary for a life of service in the Church. Pastoral knowledge acquired in the discipleship stage includes competency in the performance of liturgical roles in the seminary community as well as knowledge gained by actively participating in formation seminars. Pastoral skills adequately demonstrated by the end of the discipleship stage include relating well with others, both in the seminary and in pastoral settings; freedom from prejudices against any class or group of individuals; a willingness to work with people of diverse cultural backgrounds; demonstrated generosity to the poor given his limited means; demonstrated accompaniment of the poor; the ability to tithe; and a willingness and ability to work collaboratively as a member of a team. It is necessary that seminarians demonstrate that they relate well to women in authority and in peer situations. Seminarians demonstrate good stewardship of personal and communal property. They demonstrate the capacity to take initiative in leadership situations and express a missionary spirit with a zeal for evangelization.

375 Pastoral knowledge and pastoral skills are meaningless if they are not accompanied by pastoral charity. To aid in the development of

454 *Ratio Fundamentalis*, no. 30.

pastoral charity, it is necessary for the seminarian to demonstrate by the end of the discipleship stage a commitment to apostolic works of Christian charity and an awareness of issues surrounding global poverty.

CONFIGURATION STAGE BENCHMARKS

376 Pastoral opportunities in the seminary and in pastoral ministry allow the seminarian, with the trusting guidance of his formators, to recognize and hone his pastoral leadership skills. As a servant leader he is called constantly to look to Jesus as his model. "Jesus, the Son of God, has assumed the condition of a slave even unto death (cf. Phil 2:6-8). Before dying on the cross, he washed the feet of his disciples, commanding them to do the same (cf. Jn 13:1-17)."[455] As a human instrument of Jesus, he can demonstrate that he is articulate, good at listening, and capable of public speaking. He can take on the role of a public person in the Church. His intensive study of theology during the configuration stage is integrated with his pastoral skills and provides the intellectual tools to become an effective homilist and teacher.

377 In his pastoral assignments, the seminarian demonstrates availability to commit his life to priestly ministry, growing to demonstrate the same compassion, generosity, understanding, love for all (especially the poor), and zeal for the Kingdom that characterized the ministry of the Son of God. "This can be summed up as pastoral charity."[456] The seminarian demonstrates pastoral charity in his sensitivity and prudence with behavior and language in pastoral settings. He demonstrates multicultural sensitivity and openness to people of all ages, religious backgrounds, and social status in speech and action. He demonstrates the ability to collaborate with both men and women. He demonstrates the capacity to abide prudently by

455 *Ratio Fundamentalis*, no. 38.
456 *Ratio Fundamentalis*, no. 119.

safe environment guidelines and to maintain proper boundaries in all relationships, especially with minors and other vulnerable individuals. If a seminarian violates appropriate boundaries with adults or minors, including the sexual abuse of a minor, immediate action must be taken in accordance with diocesan or eparchial policies, the *Charter for the Protection of Children and Young People*, and Canon and civil law.

378 By the end of the configuration stage the seminarian can organize a homily around a central point. He can reflect theologically on pastoral issues. He learns that offering his life in service to the Church involves understanding and following the will of Christ in the person of his diocesan bishop or the competent authority of an institute of consecrated life or society of apostolic life. The seminarian's continued growth in confidence allows him to discern and continue to discover how God will use his unique talents in ordained ministry. Given that he will be entrusted with the temporal goods of the Church, he also demonstrates the ability to manage his own personal finances. He also remains free from unnecessary debt.

VOCATIONAL SYNTHESIS STAGE BENCHMARKS

379 As in the other stages, during this stage the pastoral dimension of formation can be presented in terms of pastoral knowledge, pastoral skills, pastoral discernment, and pastoral charity. Regarding pastoral knowledge, the deacon demonstrates "a capacity for critical observation" so that he "can discern true and false values, since this is an essential requirement of establishing a constructive dialogue with the world of today."[457] It is essential that he demonstrates the ability to celebrate the sacraments and liturgies of the Church validly, licitly, and confidently, and that he also develops a knowledge about and understanding of the role of various movements and apostolates that

457 *Ecclesia in America*, no. 40.

are so essential to the pastoral life of the Church. He understands and knows how to encourage and support consecrated life. He sees the importance of various ecclesial movements in the evangelistic life of the Church. He understands the centrality of the apostolate of Catholic education. He is open to the various unique and beautiful ways the Holy Spirit is working to bring about a new evangelization in our time.

380 The pastoral skills he demonstrates prior to ordination to priesthood include the ability to craft and successfully deliver homilies,[458] the ability to plan and execute pastoral projects, the ability to accompany engaged couples (e.g., marriage preparation) and newly married couples,[459] the ability to assist those seeking a declaration of matrimonial nullity, and the ability to work in an ecumenical and interreligious context in the United States.

381 Central to the vocational synthesis stage is learning the prudence of discernment. This discernment is twofold, both personal and pastoral.[460] Having first experienced how God leads him interiorly as he has sought his own conversion and grown in a life of prayer, the transitional deacon must now learn how God will lead him in his pastoral ministry, learning "to listen to the conscience that judges his movements and the interior urges that motivate his actions. In this way, the priest learns to govern himself using the spiritual and mental powers of mind and body. He grasps the sense of what can be done and what it would be better not to do, or what should not be

---

458 "The homily is the touchstone for judging a pastor's closeness and ability to communicate to his people. We know that the faithful attach great importance to it, and that both they and their ordained ministers suffer because of homilies: the laity from having to listen to them and the clergy from having to preach them! It is sad that this is the case. The homily can actually be an intense and happy experience of the Spirit, a consoling encounter with God's word, a constant source of renewal and growth." *Evangelii Gaudium*, no. 135. See also USCCB Committee on Clergy, Consecrated Life, and Vocations, *Preaching the Mystery of Faith: The Sunday Homily* (Washington, DC: USCCB, 2012).

459 See *Amoris Laetitia*, nos. 205-222.

460 See *Ratio Fundamentalis*, nos. 43, 120.

done."[461] Ultimately, he learns to coordinate the many obligations of his office by growing in union with Christ's pastoral charity.[462]

382 This personal discernment moves to pastoral discernment, through which the future priest learns to "listen deeply to real situations and [is] capable of good judgment in making choices and decisions." An "evangelical style of listening. . . . frees the pastor from the temptation to abstraction, to self-promotion, to excessive self-assurance, and to that aloofness, that would make him a 'spiritual accountant' instead of a 'good Samaritan.'"[463] This discernment is especially important today because of the complexity of situations in which people come needing the help of the Church. "The gaze of the Good Shepherd, who seeks out, walks alongside and leads his sheep, will form a serene, prudent and compassionate outlook in him. He will exercise his ministry with a disposition of serene openness and attentive accompaniment in all situations, even those that are most complex, showing the beauty and the demands of Gospel truth, without falling into legalistic or rigorist obsessions."[464]

383 Finally, pastoral formation must lead the transitional deacon to the desire to make a gift of his life for his people in pastoral charity, in imitation of Christ, the Good Shepherd. This will lead to an ability to convey the teachings of the Church in pastoral settings (e.g., teaching, preaching, and pastoral counseling) with charity and zeal at all times and to embrace a preferential option for the poor in pastoral settings. This desire will strengthen him, over the

461 *Ratio Fundamentalis*, no. 43.

462 "Priests who are perplexed and distracted by the very many obligations of their position may be anxiously enquiring how they can reduce to unity their interior life and their program of external activity. This unity of life cannot be brought about by merely an outward arrangement of the works of the ministry nor by the practice of spiritual exercises alone, though this may help to foster such unity. Priests can however achieve it by following in the fulfillment of their ministry the example of Christ the Lord, whose meat was to do the will of him who sent him that he might perfect his work." *Presbyterorum Ordinis*, no. 14.

463 *Ratio Fundamentalis*, no. 120.

464 *Ratio Fundamentalis*, no. 120.

years of priestly ministry, to make a generous gift of himself without counting the cost.

384 This stage, which leads to the transitional deacon's public expression of his free, conscious, and definitive intention for the priesthood, must also encourage him to find a suitable time for his spiritual preparation to priestly ordination[465] and to show his positive disposition for ongoing formation with his future brother priests after ordination.

Norms for Pastoral Formation

385 Every seminary is required to offer a coordinated program of pastoral formation that forms seminarians who are able, as shepherds of Christ's flock, to serve men and women in answering their call to holiness.[466]

386 The pastoral formation program should be an integral part of the seminary curriculum.

387 The goals and objectives of the pastoral formation program must be clearly stated and must serve as the basis for the evaluation of seminarians in this area. This statement should also include a description of professional ministerial ethics.

388 The coordinator of pastoral formation must be a priest, possess the requisite parochial experience and professional expertise, and participate in professional organizations in the area of seminary pastoral formation. The coordinator must model a love for priestly ministry in the Church.

---

465 See *Ratio Fundamentalis*, no. 77.
466 See *Lumen Gentium*, section V; *Ratio Fundamentalis*, no. 89.

389 The pastoral formation program should provide seminarians with a broad exposure to supervised pastoral service, with primary emphasis on parish ministry.

390 Determinations about the concurrent or intensive residency (onsite) program should be made by the seminary in collaboration with the ecclesiastical entity it serves. Seminaries and ecclesiastical entities that make provision for onsite experiences are also responsible for ensuring that these experiences help seminarians develop skills and attitudes that will enhance their future priestly ministry and that when ecumenical in nature—for example, clinical pastoral education (CPE)—these experiences are respectful of Catholic teaching, especially on moral or ethical issues. It is the responsibility of the competent authority to ensure that the Catholic, sacramental dimension of pastoral care is integral to all such programs in which seminarians participate.

391 Supervision, theological reflection, and evaluation are necessary components of an effective pastoral program. Although theological reflection can help the development of pastoral skills, its primary purpose is to interpret pastoral experience or activity in light of Sacred Scripture, Church teaching, personal faith, and pastoral practices. Reflection of this kind should become a lifelong habit in priestly ministry.

392 Onsite supervisors should be carefully selected with an eye to their dedication to the Church and respect for the priesthood. They should be taught the skills of pastoral supervision and evaluation. In choosing pastoral internships, summer placements and their supervisors, bishops and vocation personnel should consider carefully the particular needs of individual seminarians and the available time and supervisory skills of the supervisors.

393 In addition to onsite supervisors, others collaborating in the various ministries, as well as those served, should be asked to participate in the evaluation of seminarians in ministry.

394 The pastoral formation program should provide the seminarians with experience in working with and for the poor. Participation in ecumenical and interreligious programs of social action and outreach is also helpful.[467]

395 The program should include placements in which seminarians will experience the richness and diversity of the various cultural, racial, and ethnic groups that compose the Catholic Church in the United States. Such placements can also provide opportunities to sharpen language skills.

396 However the pastoral formation program is organized, it must pay attention to the seminarians' need to root a life of service in personal prayer. Seminarians need supervision in developing the habit of prayer in the context of pastoral activity and in learning to establish a rhythm of life that provides an appropriate balance of prayer, service, study, exercise, and leisure. Priest supervisors and mentors should be chosen who model this balance in their own life and ministry. Evaluation of seminarians in ministerial placements should include observations leading to a growing accountability in these areas.

397 The seminary should keep before its diocesan seminarians the prospect of their future incardination into a particular diocese and its presbyterate. Seminarians should have opportunities and receive encouragement to learn about their diocesan structures and offices as well as to become acquainted with the priests who compose the presbyterate.

---

467 See Second Vatican Council, *Unitatis Redintegratio*, no. 12; St. John Paul II, *Ut Unum Sint*, nos. 40 and 43.

398 During the discipleship stage, seminaries should provide a required program of apostolic activity, under the direction of a qualified coordinator who is a priest. Evaluation of seminarians should include consideration of their apostolic zeal in pastoral formation programs. They should be encouraged to understand the relationship of their apostolic activity to their personal, spiritual, and academic formation as well as their ongoing discernment of a priestly vocation.

The Ongoing Formation *of* Priests

399 The stages of priestly formation can appropriately be viewed as an initiation to sacramental life, not unlike the process envisioned in the Order of Christian Initiation for Adults. Just as the catechumen is introduced into a lifetime relationship of missionary discipleship with Jesus Christ, so too—for the one who is being formed for a lifetime of priestly service in the Church—"the term 'ongoing formation' is a reminder that the one experience of discipleship of those called to priesthood is never interrupted."[468] Sacramental preparation and initiation necessarily includes a period of postsacramental catechesis or mystagogia. Once celebrated, the sacraments are meant to be lived out, to be integrated into all dimensions of one's life, and to be a source of continuing transformation. For those who prepare for priestly ordination and for those who serve the formational process, this pattern of sacramental initiation implies the analogous necessity of helping seminarians commit themselves wholeheartedly to ongoing formation after ordination. The process and journey of the ongoing formation of priests are both necessary and lifelong. Their purpose is not only the spiritual growth of the priest himself but also the continued effectiveness of his mission and ministry. Only by continually conforming their interior lives and their ministry to the life of Jesus are priests able to live a lifetime of healthy discipleship. This cannot be done unless priests, through prayer, continue to penetrate more deeply into the mystery of Christ.[469]

400 The basic principle of ongoing formation for priests is contained in *Pastores Dabo Vobis*: "one can speak of a vocation 'within' the

468 *Ratio Fundamentalis*, no. 80.

469 "Pastoral charity demands that priests, if they are not to run in vain, should always work within the bond of union with the bishops and their fellow priests. If they act in this manner, priests will find unity of life in the unity of the Church's own mission. In this way they will be united with their Lord and through him with the Father in the Holy Spirit, and can be filled with consolation and exceedingly abound with joy." *Presbyterorum Ordinis*, no. 14.

priesthood. The fact is that God continues to call and send forth, revealing his saving plan in the historical development of the priest's life and the life of the Church and of society. It is in this perspective that the meaning of ongoing formation emerges. Permanent formation is necessary in order to discern and follow this constant call or will of God" within the context of the universal call to holiness of all disciples of Jesus Christ.[470]

401 The configuration stage and the vocational synthesis stage should lay the foundations for the ongoing formation of priests across a lifetime of ministry. This is done in several ways:

a. The seminary formation program must be imbued with a vision of life after ordination. "It is particularly important to be aware of and to respect the intrinsic link between formation before ordination to the priesthood and formation after ordination."[471]

b. Planning for ongoing formation, and learning how to plan, begins in the seminary. "Long-term preparation for ongoing formation should take place in the major seminary, where encouragement needs to be given to future priests to look forward to it, seeing its necessity, its advantages and the spirit in which it should be undertaken, and appropriate conditions for its realization need to be ensured."[472]

c. It is important that the seminary emphasize to seminarians that ongoing formation is a regular and necessary aspect of the life of priestly ministry. This conviction, imparted to the seminarians and to ecclesiastical entities alike, will encourage them to engage in the process of ongoing formation in all its dimensions—human, spiritual, intellectual, and pastoral.

d. The seminary must be vigilant that programs lead to future habits of study, prayer, and formational involvement.

---

470 *Pastores Dabo Vobis*, no. 70.
471 *Pastores Dabo Vobis*, no. 70.
472 *Pastores Dabo Vobis*, no. 70.

e. On occasion, the seminary may provide personnel and resources for transition programs into priesthood. Or it may invite newly ordained and more mature priests back to reflect on their experience of transition and to engage in mystagogical catechesis that focuses on the Rite of Ordination and subsequent experiences of ministry. The seminary could serve as a fraternal meeting point for ongoing formation.

f. The seminary may assist the transitional deacon to develop a plan of ongoing formation for his first years of priestly ministry.

402 In the United States, the seminary—in its various formational efforts—ought to lead seminarians to the vision and practice of ongoing formation contained in Canon Law[473] and in the USCCB document *The Basic Plan for the Ongoing Formation of Priests*, which is the standard for those who are ordained priests. In the latter document, the texts dealing with the newly ordained are especially important for the formational journey of priests as they begin their ministry.[474]

403 A newly ordained priest who begins his first pastoral assignment and the process of ongoing formation should expect to find the following elements:

a. Formal and informal welcoming by the diocesan bishop and presbyterate

b. A first pastor who is sensitive to the needs of the newly ordained and able and willing to offer advice and direction

c. Some group interaction with peers to reflect on the process of transition and the development of priestly identity and sources of support

473 CIC, c. 279; CCEO, c. 372.

474 "It is desirable that accompaniment by confreres of exemplary life and pastoral zeal be promoted, so that they can help young priests to experience a cordial and active participation in the life of the entire diocesan presbyterate." *Ratio Fundamentalis*, no. 83.

d. A mentor, as considered appropriate or necessary, with whom the newly ordained can reflect on ministry and life as a priest

404 The newly ordained priest should seek a spiritual director and celebrate the Sacrament of Penance regularly.

405 In the process of beginning priestly ministry and life, significant formational roles are played by the diocesan bishop, the director of ongoing formation for priests, and the entire presbyterate. In a particular way, the bishops in the United States have committed themselves to work individually in their dioceses/eparchies and, at the national level, to strengthen programs for ongoing formation and assist priests in living out their vocations in faithful and integral ways.[475] Personal accompaniment, so critical in the stages of initial formation, is just as critical throughout the lifetime of the priest. Concrete expressions of accompaniment for the priest, in addition to those listed above, include retreats and conferences, a common table, common life, and priestly associations.[476]

475 *Charter for the Protection of Children and Young People*, art. 17.
476 See *Ratio Fundamentalis*, no. 88.

Seminaries

INTRODUCTION

406 Seminaries are to be a continuation in the Church of the apostolic community gathered around Jesus.[477] This basic organizing principle means the seminary is first and foremost a learning community of the disciples of Jesus, that is, "a community of formation, wherever it is found."[478] At the same time, the seminary is a community of charity and friendship, where fraternal bonds are anchored in genuine relationships to the Lord and his Body, the Church. Finally, the seminary is a worshiping and praying community that finds its source and summit in the celebration of the Eucharist.

GOVERNANCE

407 Governance is the responsibility of the diocesan bishop or major superior.[479] To fulfill this responsibility, the diocesan bishop or major superior works in collaboration with the seminary board or boards and with others the bishop or major superior may delegate. The governing authority establishes the mission and exercises general oversight of the seminary; and it appoints the rector of the seminary, who remains in close collaboration with the board of the seminary regarding governance. The seminary should have a precise program "characterized by its being organized and unified, [and] by its being in harmony or correspondence with one aim which justifies the existence of the seminary: preparation of future priests."[480]

408 In their efforts to "organize and unify," diocesan bishops and major superiors, for their respective seminaries, ensure that the directives of the Holy See and the USCCB are fully and effectively implemented

477 See *Pastores Dabo Vobis*, no. 60.
478 *Ratio Fundamentalis*, no. 188.
479 In the case of an interdiocesan seminary, the governance pertains to the bishops involved (see CIC, cc. 243, 259, 263). However, one of the bishops may be designated the moderator of the group.
480 *Pastores Dabo Vobis*, no. 61.

through the mission, goals, and programs of the seminary; through long-range planning; through the appointment of the rector; and through seminary policies. In keeping with the principle of subsidiarity, the governing authority does not normally enter directly into the day-to-day operation of the seminary, since such duties are the responsibility of the rector.[481]

The Role of the Diocesan Bishop or Major Superior

409 The diocesan bishop or the major superior oversees the implementation of the *Decree on the Training of Priests* and this *Program of Priestly Formation*, and he ensures that the seminary statutes correspond to Canon Law. The diocesan bishop or major superior discharges these responsibilities personally and through the seminary board(s), the rector, and the rest of the seminary community. He is to visit the seminary regularly and exercise vigilance over it and the formation of his seminarians. A relationship of trust between the diocesan bishop or major superior and the rector will help to ensure that the bishop or major superior does not "undermine the Rector and other formators in the discernment of the vocations of the candidates and their adequate preparation."[482] He should encourage and support the rector and the rest of the seminary community in their dedication to this apostolate.[483] Bishops and major superiors are encouraged to be generous in offering priests to serve in seminaries who exemplify the qualities that seminarians would be well-suited to emulate.

410 The diocesan bishop or major superior ensures that the seminary offers a program in accord with the mind of the Church—including an approved written Rule of Life.

481 See CIC, c. 260.
482 *Ratio Fundamentalis*, no. 128.
483 See CIC, c. 259 §2; CCEO, cc. 336 §1, 356 §2.

411 It is essential that frequent and open communication be maintained among ecclesiastical authorities, the rector, and the rest of the seminary community to discuss the changing needs of the Church, the progress of seminarians, and developments in the seminary program.

412 At times, seminarians for the diocesan priesthood may attend seminaries owned and operated by institutes of consecrated life or societies of apostolic life and not by a diocese. In such instances, the local diocesan bishop has canonical responsibility for the welfare of all diocesan seminarians in attendance there.[484] Accordingly, he should be in regular communication with the seminary rector and be accorded a voice in the governance of the seminary.

413 The formation of seminarians preparing for the priesthood in institutes of consecrated life or societies of apostolic life is the responsibility of each institute or society and is regulated by the constitutions and other canonical legislation or directives pertaining to them, as well as by the directives of this *Program of Priestly Formation.*

414 Most seminaries sponsored by some form of consecrated life are collaborative ventures of several religious institutes or societies. Responsibility for the canonical form of governance belongs to those who hold ecclesiastical jurisdiction. The statutes of such institutions must be approved by the competent authority. The Holy See must approve priestly formation centers formed by a number of religious institutes or societies.

SEMINARY BOARDS

415 A variety of structures is legitimately used in the governance of seminaries in the United States. In situations with multiple boards, the bylaws of each should establish the clear jurisdiction and purpose

484 See USCCB Committee on Priestly Formation, *Relationship of the Local Ordinary (Bishop) to the Seminary Owned and Operated by Religious* (1981).

of each board or corporation. Care is to be taken to guarantee that the bylaws of these corporations and boards are canonically proper and in accord with civil law, providing for suitable ecclesiastical oversight.

416 An advisory board can provide a valuable service to the seminary by offering wise counsel to the diocesan bishop or major superior on governance of the seminary in accord with Church law, this *Program of Priestly Formation*, and the standards of the seminary's accrediting agency.

417 Members of the board should represent the clergy, religious, and laity who share a concern for priestly formation in all its dimensions. They should be selected from the local Churches and from the religious institutes or societies that the seminary serves. The board should reflect the multicultural composition of the Church in the region and of the dioceses or eparchies it serves.

418 Boards should have a well-articulated policy and an active practice of board development, so that board members can fulfill their responsibilities more effectively. This policy should include a provision for the regular evaluation of the board's own performance.

419 When seminary boards have fiduciary responsibility for the seminary, the members should be well prepared for that role and discharge their responsibility effectively.

FORMATION OF A GOVERNANCE POLICY

420 The process used to form governance policy[485] should be clearly defined by the diocesan bishop or major superior in consultation

485 "Governance policy" in this document refers to those norms, laws, and decrees that strictly speaking flow from the rights and obligations inherent in the authority of the diocesan bishop or major superior. Administrative policies are the responsibility of those deputed for the internal operation of the seminary, particularly the rector. Administrative policy means operational rules, regulations, and procedures that implement the mission and governance policy approved by the diocesan bishop or major superior.

with the seminary board(s) and the rector. The process should clearly identify the scope of governance authority and responsibility, while protecting the principle of subsidiarity and avoiding intrusion into administrative matters of the seminary.

421 The most important administrative policy is the mission statement of the seminary. Each mission statement must incorporate a clear understanding of and commitment to the formation of men for the ministerial priesthood. It is also important for the seminary to respond to the priorities of local Churches and the communities it serves through the establishment of appropriate policies.

422 Proposals regarding governance policy are often initiated at the level of the seminary community where concrete needs and problems occur. After review by the seminary leadership, policy proposals of major importance are presented by the rector to the seminary board and to the appropriate ecclesiastical authority, for approval and promulgation as particular legislation. Consultation of the seminary community, including seminarians themselves, should be characteristic of policy making in seminaries.

PLANNING

423 Planning provides for the long-range stability of the seminary, the effective implementation of its mission, and good stewardship of all associated resources. A realistic conception of the seminary's future should include effective planning regarding personnel, facilities, enrollment, finances, budget, and development. In their efforts to plan for the seminary's future, bishops and major superiors should enlist the assistance of the seminary board as well as the rector and other appropriate seminary leadership.

424 Sacred Scripture imposes on ecclesiastical authorities the obligation of finding worthy and faithful co-workers in the service of God's People.[486] Diocesan bishops and major superiors should encourage exemplary priests to enter the seminary apostolate and be willing to release them for such service. "Formators are needed who can ensure their full-time presence and who, above all else, are witnesses of how to love and serve the people of God, giving themselves without reserve for the Church."[487] Seminaries should cooperate with diocesan bishops and major superiors in the preparation of priest formators.[488] Deacons, consecrated men and women, and lay men and women should also be encouraged to prepare for work in seminary formation and receive assistance when appropriate. Ecclesiastical entities and seminaries must honestly plan for the financial commitment that this requires. "The presence of women in the Seminary journey of formation has its own formative significance. They can be found as specialists, on the teaching staff, within the apostolate, within families, and in service to the community."[489]

425 Facilities should be adequate to the seminary's needs and suitable for an institution of either secondary or higher education. The seminary buildings should provide an atmosphere conducive to human, spiritual, intellectual, and pastoral formation.

426 Effective formation requires other physical resources, such as libraries, laboratories, pastoral practica chapels, computer facilities, and other information technology centers.

427 Adequate enrollment is a critical component of a healthy priestly formation program. Consistently low enrollment may endanger

---

486 See 1 Tm 5:22; *Pastores Dabo Vobis*, no. 65.
487 *Ratio Fundamentalis*, no. 49.
488 "Those who are marked out to become formators need a specific preparation and generous dedication to this important task." *Ratio Fundamentalis*, no. 49.
489 *Ratio Fundamentalis*, no. 151.

the effectiveness of community life and learning. It will normally result in poor stewardship of resources and may affect the morale of the seminary community. Careful monitoring of the enrollment of qualified seminarians is critical for realistic planning. In those seminaries where enrollment has been consistently low for a protracted period, consolidation into regional or interdiocesan seminaries should be investigated.

428 A seminary must have sufficient financial resources to achieve its mission effectively, both now and in the future. The raising of annual operating income as well as endowments[490] should be planned and developed in such a way as to allow the rector to fulfill his essential role as pastor of the seminary community.[491]

STRUCTURE

429 The structure of the seminary community depends on the nature, size, model, and level of the priestly formation program. It is important that seminary structures and the responsibilities of the various members of the seminary community be clearly defined in light of the mission of the seminary. Descriptions given here should be adapted to each program.

Leadership Principles of the Seminary Community

430 All seminary leaders should be conscious that they are forming seminarians and modeling for them pastoral leadership and collaboration within a community. The exercise of authority should be clearly seen as service. Leadership is always relational:

a. It values the life and potential of each member of the community.

b. It nurtures and challenges growth in members of the community in accord with the Gospel and the Tradition of the Church.

490 See CIC, c. 264; CCEO, c. 341.
491 See CIC, c. 262; CCEO, c. 336 §2.

c. It models mature Christian behavior.

d. It values interior responsibility over simple external conformity.

e. It enables others to be of service to the community.

f. It respects and values the dignity of others.

g. It is always a ministry of love.

h. It promotes communication within the seminary community and between the seminary and the ecclesiastical entities it serves.

i. It operates by the principle of subsidiarity.

j. It follows doctrinal and canonical principles related to the sound stewardship of resources, respect for donor intent, and the observance of all social teaching and employment laws.[492]

431 Policies governing the seminary should be made by the appropriate authorities in an atmosphere of trust and understanding. While adhering to the goals of priestly formation, the leadership of the seminary community should respond appropriately to the needs and suggestions of seminarians. They should foster initiative as well as individual and group responsibility by observing the principles of subsidiarity and collaboration, while demonstrating forthright and confident leadership. Seminary leaders have a unique opportunity to serve as models for seminarians.

SEMINARY COMMUNITY LEADERSHIP ROLES

432 Seminaries may use different titles to describe necessary seminary community leadership roles. Whatever the determination of titles, the functions described below are needed for an effective priestly formation program. In keeping with the unique nature and purpose of the seminary, major posts within the seminary community are normally assigned to priests. All seminary leaders should have adequate preparation and the experience necessary to carry out the responsibilities they are assigned. They should understand the mission of the Church and seminary and be supportive of it.

492 See CIC, cc. 1267 §3, 1286 1°; CCEO, cc. 1016 §1, 1030, 1°.

433 Seminary leaders bear a special responsibility for planning, organizing, directing, and evaluating the implementation of this *Program of Priestly Formation* in their respective institutions.

Roles Within the Community of Formators

434 The community of formators must include a rector and a spiritual director.[493] The number of formators must necessarily be sufficient for, and proportionate to, the number of seminarians. Thus, often there will be more than one spiritual director, vice rector, and other priest formators as necessary to provide personal accompaniment to the individual seminarians. To provide excellent and competent priest formators, diocesan bishops and religious ordinaries should be generous in encouraging priests to prepare for seminary work or in releasing their priests for this ministry, even if the seminary is not their own.

Rector

435 The rector, always a priest, serves as the pastor of the seminary community.[494] He is to be "distinguished by prudence, wisdom and balance, someone highly competent, who coordinates the educational endeavor in the governance of the Seminary."[495] As the diocesan bishop or major superior's direct delegate for the formation of seminarians, he serves as the father in the seminary community and takes an active part in the accompaniment of seminarians throughout their formation process.

436 He sets the direction and tone of the seminary program. By creating a climate of mutual confidence and trust, he elicits the full cooperation and involvement of all members of the seminary community. His job description should be carefully drawn to ensure that he has the authority to discharge properly the responsibilities of his office. Given

493 See CIC, c. 239; CCEO, cc. 338-339.
494 See CIC, c. 262; CCEO, c. 336 §2.
495 *Ratio Fundamentalis*, no. 134.

the extent and gravity of these responsibilities, the diocesan bishop or major superior should ensure that the rector not have additional obligations outside the seminary community that detract from his primary duties.

437 The rector is appointed by the appropriate ecclesiastical authority, who, according to local statutes, seeks consultation with the seminary board and other interested parties. The rector is to make a Profession of Faith[496] and take the Oath of Fidelity at the beginning of his term. The rector is responsible to the diocesan bishop or competent authority of the institute of consecrated life or society of apostolic life and must consult with him in matters of major concern. As a rule the rector is also responsible to a seminary board, if a legal corporation exists. If the board is advisory, he should give thoughtful consideration to its counsel and take advantage of its expertise in administering the seminary. The rector continues in office until (1) a notification in writing of the lapse of a predetermined time, if the appointment was made for a specified term;[497] (2) a resignation that is validly submitted and accepted;[498] (3) legitimate removal by the competent authority for a just reason, if appointed for an indefinite period of time, according to the procedure established in the seminary's governance documents;[499] or (4) privation as a penalty for a canonical offense effected according to the norm of law.[500]

438 The rector serves as chief administrative officer and principal agent responsible for the implementation of the seminary program and Rule.[501] He should also maintain close contact with the competent authorities of the ecclesiastical entities that the seminary serves. In addition, he is often responsible for public relations and development,

496 See CIC, c. 833, 6°.
497 See CIC, cc. 184-186; CCEO, cc. 965-966.
498 See CIC, cc. 187-189; CCEO, cc. 967-971.
499 See CIC, c. 193 §3; CCEO, c. 975 §2.
500 See CIC, c. 196; CCEO, c. 978.
501 See CIC, cc. 238 §2, 260, 261; CCEO, cc. 335 §2, 338 §2.

though he may delegate these tasks to others. Although these duties may call him away from the seminary, it is important that the rector serve as leader of the internal life of the seminary both as pastor and priestly model.

439 The spiritual and personal welfare of the seminary community is a central responsibility of the rector. Regularly, the rector should give conferences to the seminary community. He should frequently preside at prayer and at the Eucharist. He is not to hear the sacramental confessions of students residing in the same house unless a student freely requests it in particular cases.[502]

440 The rector is to be carefully prepared "in sound doctrine, suitable pastoral experience and special training in spirituality and teaching methods."[503] The rector should be a model of priestly virtue, able to live himself the qualities he encourages in seminarians. A man of sound and prudent judgment, the rector should give evidence to a love of and dedication to the Church's service.

441 Depending on the size and structure of the seminary, the rector may also assume some of the responsibilities of other roles mentioned in this chapter, with the exception of the spiritual direction of seminarians.

Vice Rector

442 The vice rector, always a priest, assists the rector in areas determined by the rector and by the seminary's administrative structure. Tasks vary according to the needs of the particular seminary.[504] He must "show strong pedagogical gifts, a joyful love of the service he renders and a spirit of collaboration."[505]

---

502 See CIC, c. 985.
503 *Optatam Totius*, no. 5.
504 See CIC, c. 239 §1.
505 Congregation for Catholic Education, "Directives Concerning the Preparation of Seminary Educators," *Origins* 23:32 (January 27, 1994): no. 45. See *Ratio Fundamentalis*, no. 135.

Coordinator of Spiritual Formation

443 This priest, who must be appointed by the diocesan bishop or major superior, assists the rector by coordinating the entire spiritual formation program, giving it unity and direction.

444 The coordinator of spiritual formation makes provision for the individual spiritual direction of all seminarians and coordinates the regular visits of outside confessors to the seminary.[506] He meets regularly with the spiritual directors, providing supervision and assistance for their work.

445 Either the coordinator of spiritual formation or the coordinator of liturgy provides for the liturgical life and prayer of the seminary community, making provision for the daily celebration of the Eucharist, the Liturgy of the Hours (or the Divine Praises, in the Eastern Catholic Churches), and opportunities for celebration of the Sacrament of Penance. He is also responsible for retreats and days of recollection, making sure they are well planned and carefully executed.

Spiritual Directors

446 Seminary spiritual directors, who must always be priests and are designated for this function by the diocesan bishop or major superior,[507] are responsible for the individual spiritual direction of seminarians. Spiritual direction "is one of the privileged ways of accompanying each seminarian in discerning his vocation."[508] Those who act in this capacity should be exemplary priests who are dedicated to the Church's service and to the ministerial priesthood. They should be wise, seasoned priests and should possess some formal training in spirituality and related areas of expertise. Individual spiritual directors should continue to develop their skills and abilities through ongoing

506 *Ratio Fundamentalis*, no. 136.
507 See CIC, c. 239 §2; CCEO, c. 339 §1.
508 *Ratio Fundamentalis*, no. 136.

education programs and through inservice discussions with their fellow directors, taking care to preserve confidentiality in matters of the internal forum.

447 Since spiritual direction takes place in the internal forum, the relationship of seminarians to their spiritual director is a privileged and confidential one. Spiritual directors may not participate in the evaluation of those whom they currently direct or whom they directed in the past.[509]

Coordinator of Human Formation

448 The coordinator of human formation is a priest who coordinates the human formation program of the seminary[510] in collaboration with the rector, other members of the community of formators, professors, and specialists. He works in the external forum as an agent of the rector. The coordinator of human formation may also oversee the discipline of the seminary and the implementation of the Rule of Life. He should be exemplary for his personal maturity, pastoral experience, and appreciation of the psychological and human sciences.

449 The coordinator oversees the annual evaluation process of seminarians. The evaluation of seminarians can benefit from a team or group of priest formators assisting in the process.

450 The coordinator of human formation makes provision for psychological and counseling services in areas distinct from spiritual direction. These services are made available to seminarians for their personal and emotional development in preparation for the priesthood. The counseling given should be consistent with the policy and practice of the total seminary program. The coordinator should ensure that

509 See CIC, c. 240 §2; CCEO, c. 339 §3.
510 See *Ratio Fundamentalis*, no. 137; see also *Pastores Dabo Vobis*, nos. 43-44.

those employed as counselors for seminarians are well versed in and supportive of the Church's expectations of seminarians, including a sound understanding and acceptance of Christian anthropology.

Priest Formators

451 Priest formators monitor seminarians assigned to them in all four areas of formation, and they assist in the evaluation process. Priest formators must be exemplary in their dedication to the Church and to the ministerial priesthood. Priest formators function exclusively in the external forum and are not to engage in matters that are reserved for the internal forum and the spiritual director.

Coordinator of Intellectual Formation

452 "The intellectual formation of the candidates is the responsibility of the Rector and of the community of formators. With the participation of the 'coordinator of intellectual formation,' the formators shall ensure the cooperation of the professors and other experts, and shall meet regularly with them, in order to address teaching-related matters, so as to promote more effectively the integral formation of the seminarians."[511] It is important that the rector and the coordinator of intellectual formation ensure that intellectual coursework is understood by all members of the seminary community as formation and that it is seen as an element integral to the other dimensions of formation; it is not the only or even the primary dimension of formation.

453 In the case of collaborative seminaries, the coordinator of intellectual formation coordinates the academic work of the seminarians at the affiliated college or university.

454 The coordinator of intellectual formation, a priest, who can also be the academic dean, normally should possess a terminal degree, and

511 *Ratio Fundamentalis*, no. 141.

he assists the rector in intellectual formation, including the hiring and development of professors.

455 The coordinator of intellectual formation may be assisted by a registrar, who is responsible for maintaining the academic records of students.

Coordinator of Pastoral Formation

456 The coordinator of pastoral formation must always be a priest. He assists the rector in the pastoral formation of seminarians. This priest coordinates the pastoral activities of seminarians, so that they engage effectively in pastoral programs, reflect on their work, and gain deeper insight into the mission of the Church.

457 The coordinator provides an evaluation of the seminarians' work, calling attention to their strengths and to their potential for general and specialized ministries.

458 The coordinator provides adequate pastoral supervision for the seminarians, including the orientation and training of adjunct field education supervisors, who work directly with the seminarians in their pastoral assignments.

Specialists[512]

459 Priest formators are assisted by permanent deacons, consecrated men and women, and lay faithful who, in addition to their outstanding "human qualities and competence in their field," are people of profound faith. They provide "valuable and professional assistance" in the work of priestly formation.[513]

512 The list of specialists that follows is not meant to be exhaustive but gives description and guidance regarding some common specialist positions a seminary could employ.
513 *Ratio Fundamentalis*, no. 146.

460 Seminarians benefit from the mentorship of specialists who are permanent deacons, consecrated men and women, and laypersons.[514] Specialists serve as mentors only according to their proper expertise. They offer recommendations, opinions, and points of view to the rector and formation team, without making a formal judgment as to the suitability of the seminarians for the priesthood or advancement to the next stage of formation.[515] Seminaries should seek ways to fully integrate these mentoring relationships into the communal life of the seminary so that they have a genuine impact on the formation of the seminarians. These relationships add another facet of accompaniment to priestly formation distinct from spiritual direction and external formation advising, which are always done by priests.

Academic Dean

461 The academic dean, under the direction of the coordinator of intellectual formation, administers the academic program of the seminary in all its aspects: curriculum, courses, methods of instruction, and the academic quality and performance of professors and students.

Librarian

462 The librarian administers the library according to the standards of the respective professional accrediting and educational associations. The librarian ordinarily reports to the academic dean.

Development and Public Relations Officer

463 A person may be appointed to assist the rector with planning, communications, public relations, and fundraising. This officer makes the seminary known to the general public—especially to priests, vocation directors, schools, parishioners, and others—in an effort to attract new seminarians and gain support for the seminary.

---

514 See *Ratio Fundamentalis*, no. 143.
515 See *Ratio Fundamentalis*, no. 146.

Business Manager

464 The business manager or treasurer assists the rector in the stewardship of the financial and physical resources of the seminary.[516] The business manager or treasurer assists the rector in budget preparation and implementation as well as supervision of service personnel.[517] This individual must be an expert in financial affairs and absolutely distinguished for honesty. The business manager or treasurer administers the goods of the seminary under the authority of the rector, in accord with the budget determined by the appropriate authorities; from the income of the seminary, this specialist meets expenses that the rector or others designated by him have legitimately authorized. At the end of the year, the business manager or treasurer must render an account of receipts and expenditures to the seminary board or other legitimate authority of the seminary.[518]

465 This individual is to perform his or her duties with diligence. Specifically, this individual must do the following:

a. Be vigilant that no goods placed in his or her care in any way perish or suffer damage; to this end the business manager or treasurer is, to the extent necessary, to arrange insurance contracts.

b. Ensure that the ownership of ecclesiastical goods is safeguarded in ways that are valid in civil law.

c. Observe the provisions of Canon Law and civil law and the stipulations of the donor or lawful authority; the Church might also unjustly suffer damage if Canon and civil law are disregarded.

d. Seek accurately and at the proper time the income and produce of the goods, guard them securely, and expend them in accordance with the wishes of the rector, seminary board, or lawful norms.

e. Pay, at the proper time, the interest due by reason of a loan or pledge, and take care that in due time the capital is repaid.

516 See CIC, c. 239 §1; CCEO, c. 338 §1.

517 Given that the seminary is a juridic person in canon law (see CIC, c. 238 §1; CCEO, c. 335 §1), it is necessary for the seminary to have its own finance council or at least two counselors who assist the business manager in fulfilling his or her function. See CIC, c. 1280.

518 See CIC, c. 1284 §2, 8°.

f. With the consent of the rector or seminary board, make use of money which is surplus after payment of expenses and which can be profitably invested for the purposes of the seminary.

g. Keep accurate records of income and expenditures.

h. Draw up an account of his or her administration at the end of the year.

i. Keep in order and preserve in a convenient and suitable archive the documents and records establishing the rights of the seminary to its goods; where conveniently possible, authentic copies must be placed in the seminary archives.[519]

SEMINARY PROFESSORS[520]

Conditions of Service

466 All professors of the seminary are approved and appointed by the competent authority on recommendation of the rector according to the approved statutes of the institution.[521] To teach on an ecclesiastical faculty, a professor requires a canonical mission from the appropriate ecclesiastical authority.[522] In both cases, such commissioning represents a collaborative link between the professor and the Magisterium. "The theologian's code of conduct, which obviously has its origin in the service of the Word of God, is here reinforced by the commitment the theologian assumes in accepting his office, making the profession of faith, and taking the oath of fidelity."[523] Professors are an integral part of the mission of the seminary community. "The professors should be regarded as part of a single teaching community, and true educators. They ought to guide seminarians towards that

519 See CIC, c. 1284 §2, 1°-9°.

520 This section applies to both priests and laity who have teaching responsibilities in the seminary.

521 See *Optatam Totius*, no. 5; CIC, c. 253 §1; CCEO, cc. 340 §1, 351.

522 See *Veritatis Gaudium*, no. 27 §1; St. John Paul II, *Sapientia Christiana* (*On Ecclesiastical Universities and Faculties*, 1979); CIC, c. 818; CCEO, c. 644.

523 Congregation for the Doctrine of the Faith, *Donum Veritatis* (*Instruction on the Ecclesial Vocation of the Theologian*, 1990), no. 22, *www.vatican.va/roman_curia/congregations/cfaith/documents/rc_con_cfaith_doc_19900524_theologian-vocation_en.html*. See CIC, c. 833 7°; Congregation for the Doctrine of the Faith, Formula to be used for the Profession of Faith and for the Oath of Fidelity to assume an office to be exercised in the name of the Church (*Professio fidei et iusiurandum fidelitatis*), AAS 90 (1998): 542-551.

unity of knowledge that finds its fulfillment in Christ, the Way, the Truth and the Life."[524]

467 The professors should have advanced, preferably terminal, degrees in their teaching areas.[525] Professors in the sacred sciences, as well as philosophy, should possess a doctorate or licentiate from a university or institution recognized by the Holy See.[526] Priests who serve as professors should have appropriate experience in pastoral ministry.

468 As a general rule, professors for significant portions of the course of studies in the major theological disciplines should be priests.[527]

469 Seminaries should establish long-range plans for development of professors. These must include plans for recruiting and supporting professors, as well as plans for professors to improve their teaching skills and scholarship.

470 The nature of undergraduate study as a part of seminary formation during the discipleship stage, and the breadth of expertise required for a liberal arts education, means that the dedicated presence of many laymen and laywomen will play an especially important role at this level. By modeling a love for the Church as she is, a wholehearted fidelity to her teaching, a loyalty to the pope and bishops, an appreciation of the priesthood, and a collaborative spirit in ministry, men and women in consecrated life and laymen and laywomen who teach subjects in the sacred sciences make an important contribution to priestly formation on all levels.

471 All professors must be dedicated to the total formation of the seminarians. Professors teach first by the quality of their lives. Professors—

---

524 *Ratio Fundamentalis*, no. 142.
525 Due consideration must be given to the requirements of national or regional accrediting bodies.
526 See CIC, c. 253 §1; CCEO, cc. 340 §1, 351.
527 See *Ratio Fundamentalis*, no. 143.

that is, clerics, men and women in consecrated life, and laity—must therefore witness to the Gospel in their own lives.

472 The rector will determine the appropriate means of consulting professors in the process of evaluating seminarians.

473 Every professor influences seminarians' growth in priestly maturity. Love for the Eucharist as a source and sign of unity within the seminary program must be clearly evident in the life and attitude of professors. Therefore, regular participation in seminary liturgies is encouraged.

474 Some of the seminary professors share responsibility in all areas of the priestly formation program, including the spiritual and the pastoral formation of men. Priest professors, who also serve as spiritual directors and priest formators, should as a rule reside in the seminary (insofar as this is possible).

475 It is important to recruit well-trained and experienced professors from diverse ethnic, racial, and cultural backgrounds. This is especially important in those sections of the United States in which the Church and seminary community reflect such diversity.

476 If the seminary has a multicultural community, the professors should be encouraged to participate in programs and workshops that acquaint them with the specific situation and formational needs of their seminarians.

477 To inculcate in seminarians a sensitivity for issues of social justice, the seminary professors first must possess an awareness of the significance of questions of peace, justice, and respect for life.

478 Because of the importance of a pastoral orientation in seminary programs, some involvement by professors in parish ministry or in other apostolic activities complements their work in the seminary. Likewise, seminary professors are often called upon to help with diocesan projects and responsibilities. In this way, the seminary professors contribute to the local Church or to the religious institute or society they serve. However, the demands of the seminary are to be given priority.

Organization

479 A unity and harmony of effort should be present among all professors. To achieve this state, professors' handbooks are to outline and clearly describe expectations and responsibilities, rights, benefits, review, and grievance procedures.

480 To maintain qualified professors in accordance with ecclesiastical and professional standards, there should be a review process that regularly evaluates performance and offers direction for professional development, including participation in professional organizations. Review processes should consider the professor's teaching skills, academic competence, scholarly development (including publications), participation in professional societies, manner of life, personal dedication to the goals of priestly formation, and commitment to the Church.

481 Seminaries are expected to hold regularly scheduled meetings of the full body of professors. Both standing and ad hoc committees should regularly present appropriate and pertinent reports to the full body of professors. The leadership of the seminary and the professors should periodically discuss the seminary's mission to educate men for the ministerial priesthood in light of the Church's doctrinal understanding of the presbyteral office.

482 Together, professors should engage in a continuing evaluation of the academic programs of the seminary. This evaluation must consider the changing needs of the seminarians, the local Church in which they will serve, and the norms of higher education. To accomplish this continual renewal, professors need to be in regular communication with academic and ecclesial groups outside the seminary.

483 The seminary should provide time and financial support for seminary professors to maintain professional competence in their fields of specialization through participation in professional associations, study leaves, and sabbaticals.

484 An appropriate staff of secretaries should be provided for the professors and formators to free them for the more essential tasks of their assigned offices and for personal renewal, serious scholarship, and seminarian direction.

Doctrinal Responsibility

485 Professors must have a firm foundation in the teaching of the Church. A fundamental task of the professor is to present Catholic doctrine as formulated by the authoritative teaching office of the Church.[528]

486 The freedom of expression required by the exigencies of theological science must be respected, as well as the ability to do the research required for its progress.[529] Seminary statutes are to provide for appropriate freedom of inquiry that allows and encourages study and reflection in teaching and publishing. This freedom must be understood in the context of the purpose of the seminary and balanced by the rights of the seminarians, the institution, and the Church. "The freedom proper to theological research is exercised

528 See *Pastores Dabo Vobis*, no. 67.
529 See CIC, c. 218; CCEO, c. 21.

within the Church's faith. . . . In theology this freedom of inquiry is the hallmark of a rational discipline whose object is given by Revelation, handed on and interpreted in the Church under the authority of the Magisterium, and received by faith."[530]

487 Professors must be mindful of the varying degrees of theological certainty and must carefully distinguish between their own insights and other theological developments or opinions on the one hand and Catholic doctrine on the other.

488 Professors' handbooks should contain clear procedures for the resolution of conflicts regarding the correctness of theological expression on the part of professors in accord with existing ecclesiastical norms.[531]

530 Congregation for the Doctrine of the Faith, *Donum Veritatis*, nos. 11-12.
531 See USCCB, *Doctrinal Responsibilities: Approaches to Promoting Cooperation and Resolving Misunderstandings Between Bishops and Theologians* (1989); *Pastores Dabo Vobis*, no. 67.

Conclusion

489 The Catholic Church in the United States is deeply grateful to those dedicated to the noble enterprise of priestly formation, mindful of its cherished heritage of seminary life. Likewise, the bishops of the Church in the United States are confident that this essential task will continue in a more effective way in the ongoing years of the third Christian millennium and are firmly committed to this mission. It is their hope that this sixth edition of the *Program of Priestly Formation* will serve this goal. Christ the Good Shepherd still calls men to follow him, to "put out into deep water" (Lk 5:4), and to respond to his invitation to become a priest after his own heart, eager to be transformed through human, spiritual, intellectual, and pastoral formation.

490 May the Lord who has begun this good work among us bring it to completion.[532]

532 See Phil 1:6. See also *Ordination of a Bishop, of Priests, and of Deacons*, no. 125.

Index

THEMES

References are to paragraph numbers whenever possible. Notes are referenced by paragraph number, the letter n, and note number (282n168).

ABBREVIATIONS

Amoris Laetitia
Pope Francis, *The Joy of Love* (Washington, DC: United States Conference of Catholic Bishops [USCCB], 2016)

Catechism of the Catholic Church
Catechism of the Catholic Church, 2nd ed. (Washington, DC: Libreria Editrice Vaticana–USCCB, 2000)

Charter for the Protection of Children and Young People
United States Conference of Catholic Bishops, *Charter for the Protection of Children and Young People* (Washington, DC: USCCB, 2018)

Christus Dominus
Decree on the Pastoral Office of the Bishops in the Church, in Austin Flannery, ed., *Vatican Council II: Volume 1: The Conciliar and Post Conciliar Documents*, new rev. ed. (Collegeville, MN: Liturgical Press, 1996)

CIC
Codex Iuris Canonici (Code of Canon Law), Latin-English Edition, New English Translation, Second Printing (Washington, DC: Canon Law Society of America, 1998)

CCEO
Codex Canonum Ecclesiarum Orientalium (Code of Canons of the Eastern Churches), New English Translation (Washington, DC: Canon Law Society of America, 2001)

Compendium of the Social Doctrine of the Church
Pontifical Council for Justice and Peace, *Compendium of the Social Doctrine of the Church* (Washington, DC: Libreria Editrice Vaticana–USCCB, 2004)

Dei Verbum
Dogmatic Constitution on Divine Revelation, in Austin Flannery, ed., *Vatican Council II: Volume 1: The Conciliar and Post Conciliar Documents*, new rev. ed. (Collegeville, MN: Liturgical Press, 1996)

Ecclesia de Eucharistia
St. John Paul II, *On the Eucharist* (Washington, DC: USCCB, 2003)

Ecclesia in America
St. John Paul II, *The Church in America* (Washington, DC: USCCB, 1999)

Evangelica Testificatio
Apostolic Exhortation on the Renewal of Religious Life, in Austin Flannery, ed., *Vatican Council II: Volume 1: The Conciliar and Post Conciliar Documents*, new rev. ed. (Collegeville, MN: Liturgical Press, 1996)

Evangelii Gaudium
Pope Francis, *The Joy of the Gospel* (Washington, DC: USCCB, 2013)

Fides et Ratio
St. John Paul II, *On the Relationship Between Faith and Reason* (Washington, DC: USCCB, 1998)

Laudato Si'
Pope Francis, *On Care for Our Common Home* (Washington, DC: USCCB, 2015)

Lumen Gentium
Dogmatic Constitution on the Church, in Austin Flannery, ed., *Vatican Council II: Volume 1: The Conciliar and Post Conciliar Documents*, new rev. ed. (Collegeville, MN: Liturgical Press, 1996)

Misericordiae Vultus
Pope Francis, *Bull of Indiction of the Extraordinary Jubilee of Mercy* (Vatican City: Libreria Editrice Vaticana, 2015)

Optatam Totius
Decree on the Training of Priests, in Austin Flannery, ed., *Vatican Council II: Volume 1: The Conciliar and Post Conciliar Documents*, new rev. ed. (Collegeville, MN: Liturgical Press, 1996)

Ordination of a Bishop, of Priests, and of Deacons
United States Conference of Catholic Bishops, *Ordination of a Bishop, of Priests, and of Deacons* (Washington, DC: USCCB, 2021)

Pastores Dabo Vobis
St. John Paul II, *I Will Give You Shepherds* (Washington, DC: USCCB, 1992)

Perfectae Caritatis
Decree on the Up-to-Date Renewal of Religious Life, in Austin Flannery, ed., *Vatican Council II: Volume 1: The Conciliar and Post Conciliar Documents*, new rev. ed. (Collegeville, MN: Liturgical Press, 1996)

Verbum Domini
Pope Benedict XVI, *The Word of the Lord* (Washington, DC: USCCB, 2011)

Veritatis Gaudium
Pope Francis, *On Ecclesiastical Universities and Faculties* (Vatican City: Libreria Editrice Vaticana, 2017)

Veritatis Splendor
St. John Paul II, *The Splendor of Truth* (Washington, DC: USCCB, 1993)

Vita Consecrata
St. John Paul II, *The Consecrated Life and its Mission in the Church and the World* (Washington, DC: USCCB, 1996)